BIRDS

a spiritual journal

Record the
Symbology & Significance
of These Divine Winged Messengers

ARIN MURPHY-HISCOCK

Avon, Massachusetts

Published by
Adams Media, a division of F+W Media, Inc.
57 Littlefield Street, Avon, MA 02322. U.S.A.
www.adamsmedia.com

ISBN 10: 1-4405-2936-1
ISBN 13: 978-1-4405-2936-8

Printed in the United States of America.

10   9   8   7   6   5   4   3   2   1

Library of Congress Cataloging-in-Publication Data
is available from the publisher.

This publication is designed to provide accurate and authoritative information with
regard to the subject matter covered. It is sold with the understanding that the publisher
is not engaged in rendering legal, accounting, or other professional advice. If legal advice
or other expert assistance is required, the services of a competent professional person
should be sought.

    —From a *Declaration of Principles* jointly adopted by a Committee of the
American Bar Association and a Committee of Publishers and Associations

Many of the designations used by manufacturers and sellers to distinguish their prod-
uct are claimed as trademarks. Where those designations appear in this book and Adams
Media was aware of a trademark claim, the designations have been printed with initial
capital letters.

Albatross, Blackbird, Bluebird, Cardinal, Chickadee, Cormorant, Crane, Crow, Dove, Duck,
Eagle, Egret, Finch, Flamingo, Goldfinch, Goose, Grackle, Gull, Hawk, Heron, Humming-
bird, Ibis, Kingfisher, Lark, Loon, Mockingbird, Nuthatch, Oriole, Osprey, Owl, Parakeet,
Pelican, Pigeon, Plover, Puffin, Quail, Raven, Robin, Sandpiper, Sparrow, Stork, Swan,
Thrush, Turkey, Vulture, Waxwing, Whip-poor-will, Woodpecker, and Yellow Warbler from
120 Audubon Bird Prints, by John James Audubon, New York: Dover Publications, 2008

Blue Jay, Cuckoo, Falcon, Grouse, Magpie, Nighthawk, Petrel, Swallow, and Swift from
Audubon's Birds of America, by Roger Tory Peterson and Virginia Marie Peterson, New
York: Abbeville Press Publishers, 1981

Partridge, Wren, Starling, and Kestrel © fineartamerica.com/John James Audubon

This book is available at quantity discounts for bulk purchases.
For information, please call 1-800-289-0963.

Introduction

Birds are all around us. They inspire us, cheer us, and for ages have been celebrated as a perceived connection between our world and the realms of the unknown. Their ease in traveling between the land and highest reaches of the sky has long been seen as having special significance, and their actions have been observed and interpreted as a way to obtain illumination or insight into events.

If you're going to seriously examine birds and work to construct a personally significant method of divination in your life, you'd be well served to keep track of what kinds of birds you see and what their messages mean to you. Keeping a record is of paramount importance in a practice like this, as it allows you to return to your notes and realize the connections between the events in your life and your bird sightings.

Do you need to carry this journal with you at all times? Of course not. But do make notes as soon as you can after seeing a bird. You can use your smartphone or a scratch pad in your pocket or bag to make rough notes, and write them out in this journal later. Don't wait too long to transcribe and expand them, though; your rough notes become less useful the further away you get from the actual sighting.

How to Use This Book

How should you go about creating your own personally significant bird divination record? We've listed some key information below that you want to keep track of for each sighting. This selection of information will help you make personal choices regarding what each kind of bird means to you. Your personal history and experiences will make your encounter with a specific bird inimitable, and significantly different from the encounters other people may have with it, even if the bird is encountered in a similar setting under similar circumstances. What *you* bring to the encounter is as important as the bird's traditional associations, making your interpretation unique.

Note that not all of this information will be significant every time you have an encounter. This represents a selection of information that can be useful. You may wish to record other information as well, as the desire or inspiration strikes you.

Here's a breakdown of how to record your information.

Date and Time: It's essential to record this information if you're to observe a pattern regarding the time of day or month at which a certain bird appears to you. As a general rule, it's important to keep track of the precise time of day you saw a particular bird if you want to fine-tune the message you're receiving. For example, a bird seen in the morning can have an impact on newer projects, one seen at midday can refer to projects in full swing, and birds seen in the afternoon can refer to projects almost complete. Also, check the bird's usual hours of operation. If the bird is crepuscular, for example, and you see it at high noon, the message may be being emphasized, or it may be telling you that what it's addressing will happen sooner rather than later.

Location: Include as much information as possible here. A street address might be useful, but also use precise description, like "In the air above the intersection of Fifth and Queen, flying west," or "In the cedar hedge bordering our property and the Harris's house next door," or "In the top third of the rowan tree." Note, too, if the bird was seen flying (How high? What direction?) or perching.

The bird's natural habitat can be a clue to the message the birds have for you. Check the bird's natural habitat against where you observed it. If it was seen outside its preferred environment, it is very possible that the bird's message is being emphasized. Take note, too, of the kind of tree or bush it's in (that is, if you see it in one). Looking into the associations and correspondences the tree has can help flesh out the bird's message, or add helpful subtext.

Be sure to take the season into account as well. Some birds are migratory; others remain in their habitat all year round. Checking to see which group your bird belongs to can add dimension to the message you receive. If you're seeing a bird that should be thousands of miles away, it can be more significant than seeing one that's always around.

Weather: Was it cloudy? Was there lots of wind? Was a storm coming? Noting the weather is important for two reasons. First, you may find that certain birds appear more frequently to you in certain weather situations; second, you may discover that you're more sensitive to or aware of messages in certain environmental conditions.

Moon Phase: This may seem odd to record, but the moon does have an effect on creature behavior. Studies have suggested that the amount of light at night can affect ornithological activity, allowing diurnal birds (those that are active in the daytime) more time to fly and be active, and possibly affecting nocturnally active birds in various ways as well. Likewise, it is postulated that the physical state of various food sources such as insects or small mammals is affected by the amount of moonlight, making them more or less appealing to birds at various times of the moon cycle. On a metaphysical level, the phases of the moon have different meanings as well that can affect the message, roughly equating to expansion and growth in the first half of the cycle, and decrease or resolution in the second half. Note if the moon is dark, new, waxing, full, or waning in your journal.

What kind of bird brought you a message/had a message for you today? What kind of bird did you see? Write down your first impression as to its identification as well as a brief description of it; for reference, look at the pictures of more than sixty of the most commonly seen North American birds at the back of this journal. You might not recognize the bird at first, so jot down as many clues about its size, shape, color, and so on as possible, as those clues can be useful in later identification. If your original identification was wrong, write that down when you find out what bird it really was, too; what your mind produces as the symbol can be just as powerful as what the bird actually is.

What were you doing when you noticed the messenger? Often the bird's message can have a connection to the activity you're engaged in, either directly or via a common element between the activity and the situation the message refers to.

How were you feeling before the sighting? This provides a baseline for comparing whatever change is evoked by the bird. Also, the bird's message might pertain to the mood you were in when you saw it.

Did the sighting evoke any immediate emotions? What are your first impressions about what the bird's message might be? What is your initial emotional reaction to seeing the bird? What are your first thoughts about the import it might have, or the message it might carry? First impressions—and your own personal intuition—are extremely valuable. For most divination, you want to trust yourself; if you have a gut instinct that a bird's message references something in particular, chances are, you're correct.

What thoughts came to mind about the sighting? Were you reminded of someone special or of an event in your past? Consider the initial connections and associations that you make about the bird, its potential message, and your life. Again, first impressions are valuable. The memories stirred up or the associations made as you begin to think about the bird can offer valuable clues as to the message the bird brings. Even if the bird's message doesn't directly involve those memories or the situations featured in them, they may be linked to the theme of the message for you.

Were your feelings or mood transformed once you had the encounter? Did the sighting impact you enough to measurably change your emotional state? While this isn't necessarily a measure of how important the message is, noting what kind of change occurred can be helpful when referring to the encounter.

Are there any situations in your life that might be connected to or affected by the bird's message? Consider the situations or areas in your life that the bird's message might pertain to. Perhaps you are involved in a volatile situation or a transitional event that may be further clarified by this message.

In what way does the bird's message resonate with you? When you've had a chance to reflect on your first impressions, research the bird and think about it some more. Consider how the bird's message, both initial and researched, affects you. Could the folklore, the habits, and the spiritual symbolism of the bird speak to you and help you decipher the bird's message? Ask yourself how you think the message might apply to you and your daily life, or to a particular situation you're currently involved in. To learn more about bird divination and folklore take a look at *Birds: A Spiritual Field Guide*, this journal's companion guide to the symbology and significance of the most common birds.

Follow Up: In hindsight, how did the sighting impact you, and how was the message valuable? Leave this section of the journal blank until you've had some time to reflect on the message and its effect on your life. This time and distance may give you a better perspective on the message or how it might have been more clearly interpreted. Revisit your notes regularly, perhaps once a month, to keep them fresh in your mind and to enable yourself to see any pattern that forms.

As you begin journaling, keep in mind that recording your bird sightings is essential to constructing a meaningful relationship with this kind of living, responsive, nature-based system of divination. While the lack of an established reference system may make this type of divination frustrating at times, constructing your own personal bird reference is a wonderfully rewarding experience—one that allows you to explore and examine your own spiritual connection to the natural world. After all, the more you learn about the world around you, the more you can learn about yourself. So get ready to decipher the beautiful mysteries of our winged messengers—and learn about yourself in the process.

—*Arin Murphy-Hiscock*

Date:

Time:

Location:

Weather:

Moon Phase:

What kind of bird brought you a message/had a message for you today?

What were you doing when you noticed the messenger?

How were you feeling before the sighting?

Did the sighting evoke any immediate emotions? What are your first impressions about what the bird's message might be?

What thoughts came to mind about the sighting? Were you reminded of someone special or of an event in your past?

Were your feelings or mood transformed once you had the encounter?

_____

_____

_____

_____

Are there any situations in your life that might be connected to or affected by the bird's message?

_____

_____

_____

_____

In what way does the bird's message resonate with you?

_____

_____

_____

_____

Follow Up: In hindsight, how did the sighting impact you, and how was the message valuable?

_____

_____

_____

_____

Notes:

_____

_____

_____

_____

Date:

Time:

Location:

Weather:

Moon Phase:

What kind of bird brought you a message/had a message for you today?

_____

_____

_____

What were you doing when you noticed the messenger?

_____

_____

_____

How were you feeling before the sighting?

_____

_____

_____

Did the sighting evoke any immediate emotions? What are your first impressions about what the bird's message might be?

_____

_____

_____

What thoughts came to mind about the sighting? Were you reminded of someone special or of an event in your past?

_____

_____

_____

_____

Were your feelings or mood transformed once you had the encounter?

_____

_____

_____

_____

Are there any situations in your life that might be connected to or affected by the bird's message?

_____

_____

_____

_____

In what way does the bird's message resonate with you?

_____

_____

_____

_____

Follow Up: In hindsight, how did the sighting impact you, and how was the message valuable?

_____

_____

_____

_____

Notes:

_____

_____

_____

_____

_____

Date:

Time:

Location:

Weather:

Moon Phase:

What kind of bird brought you a message/had a message for you today?

What were you doing when you noticed the messenger?

How were you feeling before the sighting?

Did the sighting evoke any immediate emotions? What are your first impressions about what the bird's message might be?

What thoughts came to mind about the sighting? Were you reminded of someone special or of an event in your past?

Were your feelings or mood transformed once you had the encounter?

_____

_____

_____

_____

Are there any situations in your life that might be connected to or affected by the bird's message?

_____

_____

_____

_____

In what way does the bird's message resonate with you?

_____

_____

_____

_____

Follow Up: In hindsight, how did the sighting impact you, and how was the message valuable?

_____

_____

_____

_____

Notes:

_____

_____

_____

_____

Date:

Time:

Location:

Weather:

Moon Phase:

What kind of bird brought you a message/had a message for you today?

What were you doing when you noticed the messenger?

How were you feeling before the sighting?

Did the sighting evoke any immediate emotions? What are your first impressions about what the bird's message might be?

What thoughts came to mind about the sighting? Were you reminded of someone special or of an event in your past?

Were your feelings or mood transformed once you had the encounter?

_____

_____

_____

_____

Are there any situations in your life that might be connected to or
affected by the bird's message?

_____

_____

_____

_____

In what way does the bird's message resonate with you?

_____

_____

_____

_____

Follow Up: In hindsight, how did the sighting impact you, and how was
the message valuable?

_____

_____

_____

_____

Notes:_____

_____

_____

_____

_____

Date:

Time:

Location:

Weather:

Moon Phase:

What kind of bird brought you a message/had a message for you today?

What were you doing when you noticed the messenger?

How were you feeling before the sighting?

Did the sighting evoke any immediate emotions? What are your first impressions about what the bird's message might be?

What thoughts came to mind about the sighting? Were you reminded of someone special or of an event in your past?

Were your feelings or mood transformed once you had the encounter?

_____

_____

_____

_____

Are there any situations in your life that might be connected to or
affected by the bird's message?

_____

_____

_____

_____

In what way does the bird's message resonate with you?

_____

_____

_____

_____

Follow Up: In hindsight, how did the sighting impact you, and how was
the message valuable?

_____

_____

_____

_____

Notes:

_____

_____

_____

_____

_____

Date:

Time:

Location:

Weather:

Moon Phase:

What kind of bird brought you a message/had a message for you today?

What were you doing when you noticed the messenger?

How were you feeling before the sighting?

Did the sighting evoke any immediate emotions? What are your first impressions about what the bird's message might be?

What thoughts came to mind about the sighting? Were you reminded of someone special or of an event in your past?

Were your feelings or mood transformed once you had the encounter?

_____

_____

_____

_____

Are there any situations in your life that might be connected to or affected by the bird's message?

_____

_____

_____

_____

In what way does the bird's message resonate with you?

_____

_____

_____

_____

Follow Up: In hindsight, how did the sighting impact you, and how was the message valuable?

_____

_____

_____

_____

Notes:

_____

_____

_____

_____

_____

Date: _____

Time: _____

Location: _____

Weather: _____

Moon Phase: _____

What kind of bird brought you a message/had a message for you today?

_____

_____

_____

What were you doing when you noticed the messenger?

_____

_____

_____

How were you feeling before the sighting?

_____

_____

_____

Did the sighting evoke any immediate emotions? What are your first
impressions about what the bird's message might be?

_____

_____

_____

What thoughts came to mind about the sighting? Were you reminded of
someone special or of an event in your past?

_____

_____

_____

Were your feelings or mood transformed once you had the encounter?

_____

_____

_____

_____

Are there any situations in your life that might be connected to or affected by the bird's message?

_____

_____

_____

_____

In what way does the bird's message resonate with you?

_____

_____

_____

_____

Follow Up: In hindsight, how did the sighting impact you, and how was the message valuable?

_____

_____

_____

_____

Notes:

_____

_____

_____

_____

_____

Date:

Time:

Location:

Weather:

Moon Phase:

What kind of bird brought you a message/had a message for you today?

What were you doing when you noticed the messenger?

How were you feeling before the sighting?

Did the sighting evoke any immediate emotions? What are your first impressions about what the bird's message might be?

What thoughts came to mind about the sighting? Were you reminded of someone special or of an event in your past?

Were your feelings or mood transformed once you had the encounter?

_____

_____

_____

_____

Are there any situations in your life that might be connected to or affected by the bird's message?

_____

_____

_____

_____

In what way does the bird's message resonate with you?

_____

_____

_____

_____

Follow Up: In hindsight, how did the sighting impact you, and how was the message valuable?

_____

_____

_____

_____

Notes:

_____

_____

_____

_____

Date:

Time:

Location:

Weather:

Moon Phase:

What kind of bird brought you a message/had a message for you today?

What were you doing when you noticed the messenger?

How were you feeling before the sighting?

Did the sighting evoke any immediate emotions? What are your first impressions about what the bird's message might be?

What thoughts came to mind about the sighting? Were you reminded of someone special or of an event in your past?

Were your feelings or mood transformed once you had the encounter?

_____

_____

_____

_____

Are there any situations in your life that might be connected to or affected by the bird's message?

_____

_____

_____

_____

In what way does the bird's message resonate with you?

_____

_____

_____

_____

Follow Up: In hindsight, how did the sighting impact you, and how was the message valuable?

_____

_____

_____

_____

Notes:

_____

_____

_____

_____

_____

Date:

Time:

Location:

Weather:

Moon Phase:

What kind of bird brought you a message/had a message for you today?

What were you doing when you noticed the messenger?

How were you feeling before the sighting?

Did the sighting evoke any immediate emotions? What are your first impressions about what the bird's message might be?

What thoughts came to mind about the sighting? Were you reminded of someone special or of an event in your past?

Were your feelings or mood transformed once you had the encounter?

_____

_____

_____

_____

Are there any situations in your life that might be connected to or affected by the bird's message?

_____

_____

_____

_____

In what way does the bird's message resonate with you?

_____

_____

_____

_____

Follow Up: In hindsight, how did the sighting impact you, and how was the message valuable?

_____

_____

_____

_____

Notes:

_____

_____

_____

_____

_____

Date:

Time:

Location:

Weather:

Moon Phase:

What kind of bird brought you a message/had a message for you today?

What were you doing when you noticed the messenger?

How were you feeling before the sighting?

Did the sighting evoke any immediate emotions? What are your first impressions about what the bird's message might be?

What thoughts came to mind about the sighting? Were you reminded of someone special or of an event in your past?

Were your feelings or mood transformed once you had the encounter?

_____

_____

_____

_____

Are there any situations in your life that might be connected to or affected by the bird's message?

_____

_____

_____

_____

In what way does the bird's message resonate with you?

_____

_____

_____

_____

Follow Up: In hindsight, how did the sighting impact you, and how was the message valuable?

_____

_____

_____

_____

Notes:

_____

_____

_____

_____

_____

Date:

Time:

Location:

Weather:

Moon Phase:

What kind of bird brought you a message/had a message for you today?

What were you doing when you noticed the messenger?

How were you feeling before the sighting?

Did the sighting evoke any immediate emotions? What are your first impressions about what the bird's message might be?

What thoughts came to mind about the sighting? Were you reminded of someone special or of an event in your past?

Were your feelings or mood transformed once you had the encounter?

_____

_____

_____

_____

Are there any situations in your life that might be connected to or affected by the bird's message?

_____

_____

_____

_____

In what way does the bird's message resonate with you?

_____

_____

_____

_____

Follow Up: In hindsight, how did the sighting impact you, and how was the message valuable?

_____

_____

_____

_____

Notes:

_____

_____

_____

_____

_____

Date: _____

Time: _____

Location: _____

Weather: _____

Moon Phase: _____

What kind of bird brought you a message/had a message for you today?

_____

_____

_____

What were you doing when you noticed the messenger?

_____

_____

_____

How were you feeling before the sighting?

_____

_____

_____

Did the sighting evoke any immediate emotions? What are your first impressions about what the bird's message might be?

_____

_____

_____

What thoughts came to mind about the sighting? Were you reminded of someone special or of an event in your past?

_____

_____

_____

Were your feelings or mood transformed once you had the encounter?

_____

_____

_____

_____

Are there any situations in your life that might be connected to or affected by the bird's message?

_____

_____

_____

_____

In what way does the bird's message resonate with you?

_____

_____

_____

_____

Follow Up: In hindsight, how did the sighting impact you, and how was the message valuable?

_____

_____

_____

_____

Notes:

_____

_____

_____

_____

_____

Date: _____

Time: _____

Location: _____

Weather: _____

Moon Phase: _____

What kind of bird brought you a message/had a message for you today?

_____

_____

_____

What were you doing when you noticed the messenger?

_____

_____

_____

How were you feeling before the sighting?

_____

_____

_____

Did the sighting evoke any immediate emotions? What are your first impressions about what the bird's message might be?

_____

_____

_____

What thoughts came to mind about the sighting? Were you reminded of someone special or of an event in your past?

_____

_____

_____

Were your feelings or mood transformed once you had the encounter?

_____

_____

_____

_____

Are there any situations in your life that might be connected to or affected by the bird's message?

_____

_____

_____

_____

In what way does the bird's message resonate with you?

_____

_____

_____

_____

Follow Up: In hindsight, how did the sighting impact you, and how was the message valuable?

_____

_____

_____

_____

Notes:

_____

_____

_____

_____

_____

Date: _____

Time: _____

Location: _____

Weather: _____

Moon Phase: _____

What kind of bird brought you a message/had a message for you today?

_____

_____

_____

What were you doing when you noticed the messenger?

_____

_____

_____

How were you feeling before the sighting?

_____

_____

_____

Did the sighting evoke any immediate emotions? What are your first impressions about what the bird's message might be?

_____

_____

_____

What thoughts came to mind about the sighting? Were you reminded of someone special or of an event in your past?

_____

_____

_____

Were your feelings or mood transformed once you had the encounter?

_____

_____

_____

_____

Are there any situations in your life that might be connected to or affected by the bird's message?

_____

_____

_____

_____

In what way does the bird's message resonate with you?

_____

_____

_____

_____

Follow Up: In hindsight, how did the sighting impact you, and how was the message valuable?

_____

_____

_____

_____

Notes:

_____

_____

_____

_____

_____

Date: _____

Time: _____

Location: _____

Weather: _____

Moon Phase: _____

What kind of bird brought you a message/had a message for you today?

_____

_____

_____

What were you doing when you noticed the messenger?

_____

_____

_____

How were you feeling before the sighting?

_____

_____

_____

Did the sighting evoke any immediate emotions? What are your first impressions about what the bird's message might be?

_____

_____

_____

What thoughts came to mind about the sighting? Were you reminded of someone special or of an event in your past?

_____

_____

_____

_____

Were your feelings or mood transformed once you had the encounter?

_____

_____

_____

_____

Are there any situations in your life that might be connected to or affected by the bird's message?

_____

_____

_____

_____

In what way does the bird's message resonate with you?

_____

_____

_____

_____

Follow Up: In hindsight, how did the sighting impact you, and how was the message valuable?

_____

_____

_____

_____

Notes:

_____

_____

_____

_____

_____

Date: _____

Time: _____

Location: _____

Weather: _____

Moon Phase: _____

What kind of bird brought you a message/had a message for you today?

_____

_____

What were you doing when you noticed the messenger?

_____

_____

How were you feeling before the sighting?

_____

_____

Did the sighting evoke any immediate emotions? What are your first impressions about what the bird's message might be?

_____

_____

What thoughts came to mind about the sighting? Were you reminded of someone special or of an event in your past?

_____

_____

_____

Were your feelings or mood transformed once you had the encounter?

_____

_____

_____

_____

Are there any situations in your life that might be connected to or affected by the bird's message?

_____

_____

_____

_____

In what way does the bird's message resonate with you?

_____

_____

_____

_____

Follow Up: In hindsight, how did the sighting impact you, and how was the message valuable?

_____

_____

_____

_____

Notes:

_____

_____

_____

_____

_____

Date: _____

Time: _____

Location: _____

Weather: _____

Moon Phase: _____

What kind of bird brought you a message/had a message for you today?

_____

_____

_____

What were you doing when you noticed the messenger?

_____

_____

_____

How were you feeling before the sighting?

_____

_____

_____

Did the sighting evoke any immediate emotions? What are your first
impressions about what the bird's message might be?

_____

_____

_____

What thoughts came to mind about the sighting? Were you reminded of
someone special or of an event in your past?

_____

_____

_____

Were your feelings or mood transformed once you had the encounter?

_____

_____

_____

_____

Are there any situations in your life that might be connected to or affected by the bird's message?

_____

_____

_____

_____

In what way does the bird's message resonate with you?

_____

_____

_____

_____

Follow Up: In hindsight, how did the sighting impact you, and how was the message valuable?

_____

_____

_____

_____

Notes:

_____

_____

_____

_____

_____

Date:

Time:

Location:

Weather:

Moon Phase:

What kind of bird brought you a message/had a message for you today?

What were you doing when you noticed the messenger?

How were you feeling before the sighting?

Did the sighting evoke any immediate emotions? What are your first impressions about what the bird's message might be?

What thoughts came to mind about the sighting? Were you reminded of someone special or of an event in your past?

Were your feelings or mood transformed once you had the encounter?

_____

_____

_____

_____

Are there any situations in your life that might be connected to or affected by the bird's message?

_____

_____

_____

_____

In what way does the bird's message resonate with you?

_____

_____

_____

_____

Follow Up: In hindsight, how did the sighting impact you, and how was the message valuable?

_____

_____

_____

_____

Notes:

_____

_____

_____

_____

_____

Date:

Time:

Location:

Weather:

Moon Phase:

What kind of bird brought you a message/had a message for you today?

What were you doing when you noticed the messenger?

How were you feeling before the sighting?

Did the sighting evoke any immediate emotions? What are your first impressions about what the bird's message might be?

What thoughts came to mind about the sighting? Were you reminded of someone special or of an event in your past?

Were your feelings or mood transformed once you had the encounter?

_____

_____

_____

_____

Are there any situations in your life that might be connected to or affected by the bird's message?

_____

_____

_____

_____

In what way does the bird's message resonate with you?

_____

_____

_____

_____

Follow Up: In hindsight, how did the sighting impact you, and how was the message valuable?

_____

_____

_____

_____

Notes:

_____

_____

_____

_____

_____

Date:

Time:

Location:

Weather:

Moon Phase:

What kind of bird brought you a message/had a message for you today?

What were you doing when you noticed the messenger?

How were you feeling before the sighting?

Did the sighting evoke any immediate emotions? What are your first impressions about what the bird's message might be?

What thoughts came to mind about the sighting? Were you reminded of someone special or of an event in your past?

Were your feelings or mood transformed once you had the encounter?

_____

_____

_____

_____

Are there any situations in your life that might be connected to or affected by the bird's message?

_____

_____

_____

In what way does the bird's message resonate with you?

_____

_____

_____

Follow Up: In hindsight, how did the sighting impact you, and how was the message valuable?

_____

_____

_____

Notes:

_____

_____

_____

_____

_____

Date:

Time:

Location:

Weather:

Moon Phase:

What kind of bird brought you a message/had a message for you today?

What were you doing when you noticed the messenger?

How were you feeling before the sighting?

Did the sighting evoke any immediate emotions? What are your first impressions about what the bird's message might be?

What thoughts came to mind about the sighting? Were you reminded of someone special or of an event in your past?

Were your feelings or mood transformed once you had the encounter?

_____

_____

_____

_____

Are there any situations in your life that might be connected to or
affected by the bird's message?

_____

_____

_____

_____

In what way does the bird's message resonate with you?

_____

_____

_____

_____

Follow Up: In hindsight, how did the sighting impact you, and how was
the message valuable?

_____

_____

_____

_____

Notes:

_____

_____

_____

_____

_____

Date:

Time:

Location:

Weather:

Moon Phase:

What kind of bird brought you a message/had a message for you today?

What were you doing when you noticed the messenger?

How were you feeling before the sighting?

Did the sighting evoke any immediate emotions? What are your first impressions about what the bird's message might be?

What thoughts came to mind about the sighting? Were you reminded of someone special or of an event in your past?

Were your feelings or mood transformed once you had the encounter?

_____

_____

_____

_____

Are there any situations in your life that might be connected to or affected by the bird's message?

_____

_____

_____

_____

In what way does the bird's message resonate with you?

_____

_____

_____

_____

Follow Up: In hindsight, how did the sighting impact you, and how was the message valuable?

_____

_____

_____

_____

Notes:

_____

_____

_____

_____

_____

Date:

Time:

Location:

Weather:

Moon Phase:

What kind of bird brought you a message/had a message for you today?

What were you doing when you noticed the messenger?

How were you feeling before the sighting?

Did the sighting evoke any immediate emotions? What are your first impressions about what the bird's message might be?

What thoughts came to mind about the sighting? Were you reminded of someone special or of an event in your past?

Were your feelings or mood transformed once you had the encounter?

_____

_____

_____

_____

Are there any situations in your life that might be connected to or
affected by the bird's message?

_____

_____

_____

_____

In what way does the bird's message resonate with you?

_____

_____

_____

_____

Follow Up: In hindsight, how did the sighting impact you, and how was
the message valuable?

_____

_____

_____

_____

Notes:

_____

_____

_____

_____

Date:

Time:

Location:

Weather:

Moon Phase:

What kind of bird brought you a message/had a message for you today?

What were you doing when you noticed the messenger?

How were you feeling before the sighting?

Did the sighting evoke any immediate emotions? What are your first impressions about what the bird's message might be?

What thoughts came to mind about the sighting? Were you reminded of someone special or of an event in your past?

Were your feelings or mood transformed once you had the encounter?

_____

_____

_____

_____

Are there any situations in your life that might be connected to or
affected by the bird's message?

_____

_____

_____

_____

In what way does the bird's message resonate with you?

_____

_____

_____

_____

Follow Up: In hindsight, how did the sighting impact you, and how was
the message valuable?

_____

_____

_____

_____

Notes:

_____

_____

_____

_____

_____

Date:

Time:

Location:

Weather:

Moon Phase:

What kind of bird brought you a message/had a message for you today?

What were you doing when you noticed the messenger?

How were you feeling before the sighting?

Did the sighting evoke any immediate emotions? What are your first impressions about what the bird's message might be?

What thoughts came to mind about the sighting? Were you reminded of someone special or of an event in your past?

Were your feelings or mood transformed once you had the encounter?

_____

_____

_____

_____

Are there any situations in your life that might be connected to or affected by the bird's message?

_____

_____

_____

_____

In what way does the bird's message resonate with you?

_____

_____

_____

_____

Follow Up: In hindsight, how did the sighting impact you, and how was the message valuable?

_____

_____

_____

_____

Notes:

_____

_____

_____

_____

Date: _____

Time: _____

Location: _____

Weather: _____

Moon Phase: _____

What kind of bird brought you a message/had a message for you today?

_____

_____

What were you doing when you noticed the messenger?

_____

_____

How were you feeling before the sighting?

_____

_____

Did the sighting evoke any immediate emotions? What are your first impressions about what the bird's message might be?

_____

_____

What thoughts came to mind about the sighting? Were you reminded of someone special or of an event in your past?

_____

_____

_____

Were your feelings or mood transformed once you had the encounter?

_____

_____

_____

_____

Are there any situations in your life that might be connected to or affected by the bird's message?

_____

_____

_____

_____

In what way does the bird's message resonate with you?

_____

_____

_____

_____

Follow Up: In hindsight, how did the sighting impact you, and how was the message valuable?

_____

_____

_____

_____

Notes:

_____

_____

_____

_____

_____

Date:

Time:

Location:

Weather:

Moon Phase:

What kind of bird brought you a message/had a message for you today?

What were you doing when you noticed the messenger?

How were you feeling before the sighting?

Did the sighting evoke any immediate emotions? What are your first impressions about what the bird's message might be?

What thoughts came to mind about the sighting? Were you reminded of someone special or of an event in your past?

Were your feelings or mood transformed once you had the encounter?

_____

_____

_____

_____

Are there any situations in your life that might be connected to or affected by the bird's message?

_____

_____

_____

_____

In what way does the bird's message resonate with you?

_____

_____

_____

_____

Follow Up: In hindsight, how did the sighting impact you, and how was the message valuable?

_____

_____

_____

_____

Notes:

_____

_____

_____

_____

_____

Date: _____

Time: _____

Location: _____

Weather: _____

Moon Phase: _____

What kind of bird brought you a message/had a message for you today?

_____

_____

_____

What were you doing when you noticed the messenger?

_____

_____

_____

How were you feeling before the sighting?

_____

_____

_____

Did the sighting evoke any immediate emotions? What are your first impressions about what the bird's message might be?

_____

_____

_____

What thoughts came to mind about the sighting? Were you reminded of someone special or of an event in your past?

_____

_____

_____

Were your feelings or mood transformed once you had the encounter?

_____

_____

_____

_____

Are there any situations in your life that might be connected to or affected by the bird's message?

_____

_____

_____

_____

In what way does the bird's message resonate with you?

_____

_____

_____

_____

Follow Up: In hindsight, how did the sighting impact you, and how was the message valuable?

_____

_____

_____

_____

Notes:

_____

_____

_____

_____

Date:

Time:

Location:

Weather:

Moon Phase:

What kind of bird brought you a message/had a message for you today?

What were you doing when you noticed the messenger?

How were you feeling before the sighting?

Did the sighting evoke any immediate emotions? What are your first impressions about what the bird's message might be?

What thoughts came to mind about the sighting? Were you reminded of someone special or of an event in your past?

Were your feelings or mood transformed once you had the encounter?

_____

_____

_____

_____

Are there any situations in your life that might be connected to or affected by the bird's message?

_____

_____

_____

_____

In what way does the bird's message resonate with you?

_____

_____

_____

_____

Follow Up: In hindsight, how did the sighting impact you, and how was the message valuable?

_____

_____

_____

_____

Notes:

_____

_____

_____

_____

_____

Date: _____

Time: _____

Location: _____

Weather: _____

Moon Phase: _____

What kind of bird brought you a message/had a message for you today?

_____

_____

_____

What were you doing when you noticed the messenger?

_____

_____

_____

How were you feeling before the sighting?

_____

_____

_____

Did the sighting evoke any immediate emotions? What are your first impressions about what the bird's message might be?

_____

_____

_____

What thoughts came to mind about the sighting? Were you reminded of someone special or of an event in your past?

_____

_____

_____

Were your feelings or mood transformed once you had the encounter?

_____

_____

_____

_____

Are there any situations in your life that might be connected to or affected by the bird's message?

_____

_____

_____

_____

In what way does the bird's message resonate with you?

_____

_____

_____

_____

Follow Up: In hindsight, how did the sighting impact you, and how was the message valuable?

_____

_____

_____

_____

Notes:

_____

_____

_____

_____

_____

Date:

Time:

Location:

Weather:

Moon Phase:

What kind of bird brought you a message/had a message for you today?

What were you doing when you noticed the messenger?

How were you feeling before the sighting?

Did the sighting evoke any immediate emotions? What are your first impressions about what the bird's message might be?

What thoughts came to mind about the sighting? Were you reminded of someone special or of an event in your past?

Were your feelings or mood transformed once you had the encounter?

_____

_____

_____

_____

Are there any situations in your life that might be connected to or affected by the bird's message?

_____

_____

_____

_____

In what way does the bird's message resonate with you?

_____

_____

_____

_____

Follow Up: In hindsight, how did the sighting impact you, and how was the message valuable?

_____

_____

_____

_____

Notes:
_____

_____

_____

_____

_____

Date:

Time:

Location:

Weather:

Moon Phase:

What kind of bird brought you a message/had a message for you today?

What were you doing when you noticed the messenger?

How were you feeling before the sighting?

Did the sighting evoke any immediate emotions? What are your first impressions about what the bird's message might be?

What thoughts came to mind about the sighting? Were you reminded of someone special or of an event in your past?

Were your feelings or mood transformed once you had the encounter?

_____

_____

_____

_____

Are there any situations in your life that might be connected to or affected by the bird's message?

_____

_____

_____

_____

In what way does the bird's message resonate with you?

_____

_____

_____

_____

Follow Up: In hindsight, how did the sighting impact you, and how was the message valuable?

_____

_____

_____

_____

Notes:

_____

_____

_____

_____

_____

Date:

Time:

Location:

Weather:

Moon Phase:

What kind of bird brought you a message/had a message for you today?

What were you doing when you noticed the messenger?

How were you feeling before the sighting?

Did the sighting evoke any immediate emotions? What are your first impressions about what the bird's message might be?

What thoughts came to mind about the sighting? Were you reminded of someone special or of an event in your past?

Were your feelings or mood transformed once you had the encounter?

_____

_____

_____

_____

Are there any situations in your life that might be connected to or affected by the bird's message?

_____

_____

_____

In what way does the bird's message resonate with you?

_____

_____

_____

Follow Up: In hindsight, how did the sighting impact you, and how was the message valuable?

_____

_____

_____

Notes:

_____

_____

_____

_____

_____

Date:

Time:

Location:

Weather:

Moon Phase:

What kind of bird brought you a message/had a message for you today?

What were you doing when you noticed the messenger?

How were you feeling before the sighting?

Did the sighting evoke any immediate emotions? What are your first impressions about what the bird's message might be?

What thoughts came to mind about the sighting? Were you reminded of someone special or of an event in your past?

Were your feelings or mood transformed once you had the encounter?

_____

_____

_____

_____

Are there any situations in your life that might be connected to or affected by the bird's message?

_____

_____

_____

_____

In what way does the bird's message resonate with you?

_____

_____

_____

_____

Follow Up: In hindsight, how did the sighting impact you, and how was the message valuable?

_____

_____

_____

_____

Notes:

_____

_____

_____

_____

_____

Date:

Time:

Location:

Weather:

Moon Phase:

What kind of bird brought you a message/had a message for you today?

What were you doing when you noticed the messenger?

How were you feeling before the sighting?

Did the sighting evoke any immediate emotions? What are your first impressions about what the bird's message might be?

What thoughts came to mind about the sighting? Were you reminded of someone special or of an event in your past?

Were your feelings or mood transformed once you had the encounter?

_____

_____

_____

_____

Are there any situations in your life that might be connected to or affected by the bird's message?

_____

_____

_____

_____

In what way does the bird's message resonate with you?

_____

_____

_____

_____

Follow Up: In hindsight, how did the sighting impact you, and how was the message valuable?

_____

_____

_____

_____

Notes:

_____

_____

_____

_____

_____

Date:

Time:

Location:

Weather:

Moon Phase:

What kind of bird brought you a message/had a message for you today?

What were you doing when you noticed the messenger?

How were you feeling before the sighting?

Did the sighting evoke any immediate emotions? What are your first impressions about what the bird's message might be?

What thoughts came to mind about the sighting? Were you reminded of someone special or of an event in your past?

Were your feelings or mood transformed once you had the encounter?

_____

_____

_____

_____

Are there any situations in your life that might be connected to or affected by the bird's message?

_____

_____

_____

_____

In what way does the bird's message resonate with you?

_____

_____

_____

Follow Up: In hindsight, how did the sighting impact you, and how was the message valuable?

_____

_____

_____

_____

Notes:

_____

_____

_____

_____

_____

Date: _____

Time: _____

Location: _____

Weather: _____

Moon Phase: _____

What kind of bird brought you a message/had a message for you today?

_____

_____

What were you doing when you noticed the messenger?

_____

_____

How were you feeling before the sighting?

_____

_____

Did the sighting evoke any immediate emotions? What are your first impressions about what the bird's message might be?

_____

_____

What thoughts came to mind about the sighting? Were you reminded of someone special or of an event in your past?

_____

_____

_____

Were your feelings or mood transformed once you had the encounter?

_____

_____

_____

_____

Are there any situations in your life that might be connected to or affected by the bird's message?

_____

_____

_____

_____

In what way does the bird's message resonate with you?

_____

_____

_____

_____

Follow Up: In hindsight, how did the sighting impact you, and how was the message valuable?

_____

_____

_____

_____

Notes:

_____

_____

_____

_____

_____

Date:

Time:

Location:

Weather:

Moon Phase:

What kind of bird brought you a message/had a message for you today?

What were you doing when you noticed the messenger?

How were you feeling before the sighting?

Did the sighting evoke any immediate emotions? What are your first impressions about what the bird's message might be?

What thoughts came to mind about the sighting? Were you reminded of someone special or of an event in your past?

Were your feelings or mood transformed once you had the encounter?

_____

_____

_____

_____

Are there any situations in your life that might be connected to or affected by the bird's message?

_____

_____

_____

_____

In what way does the bird's message resonate with you?

_____

_____

_____

_____

Follow Up: In hindsight, how did the sighting impact you, and how was the message valuable?

_____

_____

_____

_____

Notes:

_____

_____

_____

_____

_____

Date:

Time:

Location:

Weather:

Moon Phase:

What kind of bird brought you a message/had a message for you today?

What were you doing when you noticed the messenger?

How were you feeling before the sighting?

Did the sighting evoke any immediate emotions? What are your first impressions about what the bird's message might be?

What thoughts came to mind about the sighting? Were you reminded of someone special or of an event in your past?

Were your feelings or mood transformed once you had the encounter?

_____

_____

_____

_____

Are there any situations in your life that might be connected to or affected by the bird's message?

_____

_____

_____

_____

In what way does the bird's message resonate with you?

_____

_____

_____

_____

Follow Up: In hindsight, how did the sighting impact you, and how was the message valuable?

_____

_____

_____

_____

Notes:

_____

_____

_____

_____

_____

Date: _____

Time: _____

Location: _____

Weather: _____

Moon Phase: _____

What kind of bird brought you a message/had a message for you today?

_____

_____

_____

What were you doing when you noticed the messenger?

_____

_____

_____

How were you feeling before the sighting?

_____

_____

_____

Did the sighting evoke any immediate emotions? What are your first impressions about what the bird's message might be?

_____

_____

_____

What thoughts came to mind about the sighting? Were you reminded of someone special or of an event in your past?

_____

_____

_____

Were your feelings or mood transformed once you had the encounter?

_____

_____

_____

_____

Are there any situations in your life that might be connected to or affected by the bird's message?

_____

_____

_____

_____

In what way does the bird's message resonate with you?

_____

_____

_____

_____

Follow Up: In hindsight, how did the sighting impact you, and how was the message valuable?

_____

_____

_____

_____

Notes:

_____

_____

_____

_____

Date:

Time:

Location:

Weather:

Moon Phase:

What kind of bird brought you a message/had a message for you today?

What were you doing when you noticed the messenger?

How were you feeling before the sighting?

Did the sighting evoke any immediate emotions? What are your first impressions about what the bird's message might be?

What thoughts came to mind about the sighting? Were you reminded of someone special or of an event in your past?

Were your feelings or mood transformed once you had the encounter?

_____

_____

_____

_____

Are there any situations in your life that might be connected to or affected by the bird's message?

_____

_____

_____

_____

In what way does the bird's message resonate with you?

_____

_____

_____

_____

Follow Up: In hindsight, how did the sighting impact you, and how was the message valuable?

_____

_____

_____

_____

Notes:

_____

_____

_____

_____

_____

Date:

Time:

Location:

Weather:

Moon Phase:

What kind of bird brought you a message/had a message for you today?

_____

_____

_____

What were you doing when you noticed the messenger?

_____

_____

_____

How were you feeling before the sighting?

_____

_____

_____

Did the sighting evoke any immediate emotions? What are your first impressions about what the bird's message might be?

_____

_____

_____

What thoughts came to mind about the sighting? Were you reminded of someone special or of an event in your past?

_____

_____

_____

Were your feelings or mood transformed once you had the encounter?

_____

_____

_____

_____

Are there any situations in your life that might be connected to or affected by the bird's message?

_____

_____

_____

_____

In what way does the bird's message resonate with you?

_____

_____

_____

_____

Follow Up: In hindsight, how did the sighting impact you, and how was the message valuable?

_____

_____

_____

_____

Notes:

_____

_____

_____

_____

_____

Date:

Time:

Location:

Weather:

Moon Phase:

What kind of bird brought you a message/had a message for you today?

What were you doing when you noticed the messenger?

How were you feeling before the sighting?

Did the sighting evoke any immediate emotions? What are your first impressions about what the bird's message might be?

What thoughts came to mind about the sighting? Were you reminded of someone special or of an event in your past?

Were your feelings or mood transformed once you had the encounter?

_____

_____

_____

_____

Are there any situations in your life that might be connected to or affected by the bird's message?

_____

_____

_____

_____

In what way does the bird's message resonate with you?

_____

_____

_____

_____

Follow Up: In hindsight, how did the sighting impact you, and how was the message valuable?

_____

_____

_____

_____

Notes:

_____

_____

_____

_____

_____

Date:

Time:

Location:

Weather:

Moon Phase:

What kind of bird brought you a message/had a message for you today?

What were you doing when you noticed the messenger?

How were you feeling before the sighting?

Did the sighting evoke any immediate emotions? What are your first impressions about what the bird's message might be?

What thoughts came to mind about the sighting? Were you reminded of someone special or of an event in your past?

Were your feelings or mood transformed once you had the encounter?

_____

_____

_____

_____

Are there any situations in your life that might be connected to or affected by the bird's message?

_____

_____

_____

_____

In what way does the bird's message resonate with you?

_____

_____

_____

_____

Follow Up: In hindsight, how did the sighting impact you, and how was the message valuable?

_____

_____

_____

_____

Notes:

_____

_____

_____

_____

_____

_____

Date:

Time:

Location:

Weather:

Moon Phase:

What kind of bird brought you a message/had a message for you today?

What were you doing when you noticed the messenger?

How were you feeling before the sighting?

Did the sighting evoke any immediate emotions? What are your first impressions about what the bird's message might be?

What thoughts came to mind about the sighting? Were you reminded of someone special or of an event in your past?

Were your feelings or mood transformed once you had the encounter?

_____

_____

_____

_____

Are there any situations in your life that might be connected to or affected by the bird's message?

_____

_____

_____

_____

In what way does the bird's message resonate with you?

_____

_____

_____

_____

Follow Up: In hindsight, how did the sighting impact you, and how was the message valuable?

_____

_____

_____

_____

Notes:

_____

_____

_____

_____

_____

Date:

Time:

Location:

Weather:

Moon Phase:

What kind of bird brought you a message/had a message for you today?

What were you doing when you noticed the messenger?

How were you feeling before the sighting?

Did the sighting evoke any immediate emotions? What are your first impressions about what the bird's message might be?

What thoughts came to mind about the sighting? Were you reminded of someone special or of an event in your past?

Were your feelings or mood transformed once you had the encounter?

_____

_____

_____

_____

Are there any situations in your life that might be connected to or affected by the bird's message?

_____

_____

_____

_____

In what way does the bird's message resonate with you?

_____

_____

_____

_____

Follow Up: In hindsight, how did the sighting impact you, and how was the message valuable?

_____

_____

_____

_____

Notes:

_____

_____

_____

_____

_____

Date:

Time:

Location:

Weather:

Moon Phase:

What kind of bird brought you a message/had a message for you today?

What were you doing when you noticed the messenger?

How were you feeling before the sighting?

Did the sighting evoke any immediate emotions? What are your first impressions about what the bird's message might be?

What thoughts came to mind about the sighting? Were you reminded of someone special or of an event in your past?

Were your feelings or mood transformed once you had the encounter?

_____

_____

_____

_____

Are there any situations in your life that might be connected to or affected by the bird's message?

_____

_____

_____

_____

In what way does the bird's message resonate with you?

_____

_____

_____

_____

Follow Up: In hindsight, how did the sighting impact you, and how was the message valuable?

_____

_____

_____

_____

Notes:

_____

_____

_____

_____

_____

Date:

Time:

Location:

Weather:

Moon Phase:

What kind of bird brought you a message/had a message for you today?

What were you doing when you noticed the messenger?

How were you feeling before the sighting?

Did the sighting evoke any immediate emotions? What are your first impressions about what the bird's message might be?

What thoughts came to mind about the sighting? Were you reminded of someone special or of an event in your past?

Were your feelings or mood transformed once you had the encounter?

_____

_____

_____

_____

Are there any situations in your life that might be connected to or affected by the bird's message?

_____

_____

_____

_____

In what way does the bird's message resonate with you?

_____

_____

_____

_____

Follow Up: In hindsight, how did the sighting impact you, and how was the message valuable?

_____

_____

_____

_____

Notes:

_____

_____

_____

_____

_____

Date:

Time:

Location:

Weather:

Moon Phase:

What kind of bird brought you a message/had a message for you today?

What were you doing when you noticed the messenger?

How were you feeling before the sighting?

Did the sighting evoke any immediate emotions? What are your first impressions about what the bird's message might be?

What thoughts came to mind about the sighting? Were you reminded of someone special or of an event in your past?

Were your feelings or mood transformed once you had the encounter?

_____

_____

_____

_____

Are there any situations in your life that might be connected to or affected by the bird's message?

_____

_____

_____

_____

In what way does the bird's message resonate with you?

_____

_____

_____

_____

Follow Up: In hindsight, how did the sighting impact you, and how was the message valuable?

_____

_____

_____

_____

Notes:

_____

_____

_____

_____

Date:

Time:

Location:

Weather:

Moon Phase:

What kind of bird brought you a message/had a message for you today?

What were you doing when you noticed the messenger?

How were you feeling before the sighting?

Did the sighting evoke any immediate emotions? What are your first impressions about what the bird's message might be?

What thoughts came to mind about the sighting? Were you reminded of someone special or of an event in your past?

Were your feelings or mood transformed once you had the encounter?

_____

_____

_____

_____

Are there any situations in your life that might be connected to or affected by the bird's message?

_____

_____

_____

_____

In what way does the bird's message resonate with you?

_____

_____

_____

_____

Follow Up: In hindsight, how did the sighting impact you, and how was the message valuable?

_____

_____

_____

_____

Notes:

_____

_____

_____

_____

_____

Date:

Time:

Location:

Weather:

Moon Phase:

What kind of bird brought you a message/had a message for you today?

What were you doing when you noticed the messenger?

How were you feeling before the sighting?

Did the sighting evoke any immediate emotions? What are your first impressions about what the bird's message might be?

What thoughts came to mind about the sighting? Were you reminded of someone special or of an event in your past?

Were your feelings or mood transformed once you had the encounter?

_____

_____

_____

_____

Are there any situations in your life that might be connected to or affected by the bird's message?

_____

_____

_____

_____

In what way does the bird's message resonate with you?

_____

_____

_____

_____

Follow Up: In hindsight, how did the sighting impact you, and how was the message valuable?

_____

_____

_____

_____

Notes:

_____

_____

_____

_____

_____

Date:

Time:

Location:

Weather:

Moon Phase:

What kind of bird brought you a message/had a message for you today?

What were you doing when you noticed the messenger?

How were you feeling before the sighting?

Did the sighting evoke any immediate emotions? What are your first impressions about what the bird's message might be?

What thoughts came to mind about the sighting? Were you reminded of someone special or of an event in your past?

Were your feelings or mood transformed once you had the encounter?

_____

_____

_____

_____

Are there any situations in your life that might be connected to or affected by the bird's message?

_____

_____

_____

_____

In what way does the bird's message resonate with you?

_____

_____

_____

_____

Follow Up: In hindsight, how did the sighting impact you, and how was the message valuable?

_____

_____

_____

_____

Notes:

_____

_____

_____

_____

_____

Date:

Time:

Location:

Weather:

Moon Phase:

What kind of bird brought you a message/had a message for you today?

What were you doing when you noticed the messenger?

How were you feeling before the sighting?

Did the sighting evoke any immediate emotions? What are your first impressions about what the bird's message might be?

What thoughts came to mind about the sighting? Were you reminded of someone special or of an event in your past?

Were your feelings or mood transformed once you had the encounter?

_____

_____

_____

_____

Are there any situations in your life that might be connected to or affected by the bird's message?

_____

_____

_____

_____

In what way does the bird's message resonate with you?

_____

_____

_____

_____

Follow Up: In hindsight, how did the sighting impact you, and how was the message valuable?

_____

_____

_____

_____

Notes:

_____

_____

_____

_____

_____

Date:

Time:

Location:

Weather:

Moon Phase:

What kind of bird brought you a message/had a message for you today?

What were you doing when you noticed the messenger?

How were you feeling before the sighting?

Did the sighting evoke any immediate emotions? What are your first impressions about what the bird's message might be?

What thoughts came to mind about the sighting? Were you reminded of someone special or of an event in your past?

Were your feelings or mood transformed once you had the encounter?

_____

_____

_____

_____

Are there any situations in your life that might be connected to or affected by the bird's message?

_____

_____

_____

_____

In what way does the bird's message resonate with you?

_____

_____

_____

_____

Follow Up: In hindsight, how did the sighting impact you, and how was the message valuable?

_____

_____

_____

_____

Notes:

_____

_____

_____

_____

_____

Date:

Time:

Location:

Weather:

Moon Phase:

What kind of bird brought you a message/had a message for you today?

What were you doing when you noticed the messenger?

How were you feeling before the sighting?

Did the sighting evoke any immediate emotions? What are your first impressions about what the bird's message might be?

What thoughts came to mind about the sighting? Were you reminded of someone special or of an event in your past?

Were your feelings or mood transformed once you had the encounter?

_____

_____

_____

_____

Are there any situations in your life that might be connected to or affected by the bird's message?

_____

_____

_____

_____

In what way does the bird's message resonate with you?

_____

_____

_____

_____

Follow Up: In hindsight, how did the sighting impact you, and how was the message valuable?

_____

_____

_____

_____

Notes:

_____

_____

_____

_____

_____

Date:

Time:

Location:

Weather:

Moon Phase:

What kind of bird brought you a message/had a message for you today?

What were you doing when you noticed the messenger?

How were you feeling before the sighting?

Did the sighting evoke any immediate emotions? What are your first impressions about what the bird's message might be?

What thoughts came to mind about the sighting? Were you reminded of someone special or of an event in your past?

Were your feelings or mood transformed once you had the encounter?

_____

_____

_____

_____

Are there any situations in your life that might be connected to or affected by the bird's message?

_____

_____

_____

_____

In what way does the bird's message resonate with you?

_____

_____

_____

_____

Follow Up: In hindsight, how did the sighting impact you, and how was the message valuable?

_____

_____

_____

_____

Notes:

_____

_____

_____

_____

_____

Date:

Time:

Location:

Weather:

Moon Phase:

What kind of bird brought you a message/had a message for you today?

What were you doing when you noticed the messenger?

How were you feeling before the sighting?

Did the sighting evoke any immediate emotions? What are your first impressions about what the bird's message might be?

What thoughts came to mind about the sighting? Were you reminded of someone special or of an event in your past?

Were your feelings or mood transformed once you had the encounter?

_____

_____

_____

Are there any situations in your life that might be connected to or
affected by the bird's message?

_____

_____

_____

In what way does the bird's message resonate with you?

_____

_____

_____

Follow Up: In hindsight, how did the sighting impact you, and how was
the message valuable?

_____

_____

_____

Notes:

_____

_____

_____

_____

Date:

Time:

Location:

Weather:

Moon Phase:

What kind of bird brought you a message/had a message for you today?

_____

_____

_____

What were you doing when you noticed the messenger?

_____

_____

_____

How were you feeling before the sighting?

_____

_____

_____

Did the sighting evoke any immediate emotions? What are your first impressions about what the bird's message might be?

_____

_____

_____

What thoughts came to mind about the sighting? Were you reminded of someone special or of an event in your past?

_____

_____

_____

Were your feelings or mood transformed once you had the encounter?

_____

_____

_____

_____

Are there any situations in your life that might be connected to or affected by the bird's message?

_____

_____

_____

_____

In what way does the bird's message resonate with you?

_____

_____

_____

_____

Follow Up: In hindsight, how did the sighting impact you, and how was the message valuable?

_____

_____

_____

_____

Notes:

_____

_____

_____

_____

_____

Date: _____

Time: _____

Location: _____

Weather: _____

Moon Phase: _____

What kind of bird brought you a message/had a message for you today?

_____

_____

_____

What were you doing when you noticed the messenger?

_____

_____

_____

How were you feeling before the sighting?

_____

_____

_____

Did the sighting evoke any immediate emotions? What are your first impressions about what the bird's message might be?

_____

_____

_____

What thoughts came to mind about the sighting? Were you reminded of someone special or of an event in your past?

_____

_____

_____

_____

Were your feelings or mood transformed once you had the encounter?

_____

_____

_____

_____

Are there any situations in your life that might be connected to or affected by the bird's message?

_____

_____

_____

_____

In what way does the bird's message resonate with you?

_____

_____

_____

_____

Follow Up: In hindsight, how did the sighting impact you, and how was the message valuable?

_____

_____

_____

_____

Notes:

_____

_____

_____

_____

_____

Date:

Time:

Location:

Weather:

Moon Phase:

What kind of bird brought you a message/had a message for you today?

What were you doing when you noticed the messenger?

How were you feeling before the sighting?

Did the sighting evoke any immediate emotions? What are your first impressions about what the bird's message might be?

What thoughts came to mind about the sighting? Were you reminded of someone special or of an event in your past?

Were your feelings or mood transformed once you had the encounter?

_____

_____

_____

_____

Are there any situations in your life that might be connected to or affected by the bird's message?

_____

_____

_____

_____

In what way does the bird's message resonate with you?

_____

_____

_____

_____

Follow Up: In hindsight, how did the sighting impact you, and how was the message valuable?

_____

_____

_____

_____

Notes:

_____

_____

_____

_____

_____

Date: _____

Time: _____

Location: _____

Weather: _____

Moon Phase: _____

What kind of bird brought you a message/had a message for you today?

_____

_____

_____

What were you doing when you noticed the messenger?

_____

_____

_____

How were you feeling before the sighting?

_____

_____

_____

Did the sighting evoke any immediate emotions? What are your first impressions about what the bird's message might be?

_____

_____

_____

What thoughts came to mind about the sighting? Were you reminded of someone special or of an event in your past?

_____

_____

_____

Were your feelings or mood transformed once you had the encounter?

_____

_____

_____

_____

Are there any situations in your life that might be connected to or affected by the bird's message?

_____

_____

_____

_____

In what way does the bird's message resonate with you?

_____

_____

_____

_____

Follow Up: In hindsight, how did the sighting impact you, and how was the message valuable?

_____

_____

_____

_____

Notes:

_____

_____

_____

_____

_____

Date:

Time:

Location:

Weather:

Moon Phase:

What kind of bird brought you a message/had a message for you today?

What were you doing when you noticed the messenger?

How were you feeling before the sighting?

Did the sighting evoke any immediate emotions? What are your first impressions about what the bird's message might be?

What thoughts came to mind about the sighting? Were you reminded of someone special or of an event in your past?

Were your feelings or mood transformed once you had the encounter?

_____

_____

_____

_____

Are there any situations in your life that might be connected to or affected by the bird's message?

_____

_____

_____

_____

In what way does the bird's message resonate with you?

_____

_____

_____

_____

Follow Up: In hindsight, how did the sighting impact you, and how was the message valuable?

_____

_____

_____

_____

Notes:

_____

_____

_____

_____

_____

Date:

Time:

Location:

Weather:

Moon Phase:

What kind of bird brought you a message/had a message for you today?

What were you doing when you noticed the messenger?

How were you feeling before the sighting?

Did the sighting evoke any immediate emotions? What are your first impressions about what the bird's message might be?

What thoughts came to mind about the sighting? Were you reminded of someone special or of an event in your past?

Were your feelings or mood transformed once you had the encounter?

_____

_____

_____

_____

Are there any situations in your life that might be connected to or affected by the bird's message?

_____

_____

_____

_____

In what way does the bird's message resonate with you?

_____

_____

_____

_____

Follow Up: In hindsight, how did the sighting impact you, and how was the message valuable?

_____

_____

_____

_____

Notes:

_____

_____

_____

_____

_____

Date:

Time:

Location:

Weather:

Moon Phase:

What kind of bird brought you a message/had a message for you today?

What were you doing when you noticed the messenger?

How were you feeling before the sighting?

Did the sighting evoke any immediate emotions? What are your first impressions about what the bird's message might be?

What thoughts came to mind about the sighting? Were you reminded of someone special or of an event in your past?

Were your feelings or mood transformed once you had the encounter?

_____

_____

_____

_____

Are there any situations in your life that might be connected to or
affected by the bird's message?

_____

_____

_____

_____

In what way does the bird's message resonate with you?

_____

_____

_____

_____

Follow Up: In hindsight, how did the sighting impact you, and how was
the message valuable?

_____

_____

_____

_____

Notes:

_____

_____

_____

_____

_____

Date:

Time:

Location:

Weather:

Moon Phase:

What kind of bird brought you a message/had a message for you today?

What were you doing when you noticed the messenger?

How were you feeling before the sighting?

Did the sighting evoke any immediate emotions? What are your first impressions about what the bird's message might be?

What thoughts came to mind about the sighting? Were you reminded of someone special or of an event in your past?

Were your feelings or mood transformed once you had the encounter?

_____

_____

_____

_____

Are there any situations in your life that might be connected to or affected by the bird's message?

_____

_____

_____

_____

In what way does the bird's message resonate with you?

_____

_____

_____

_____

Follow Up: In hindsight, how did the sighting impact you, and how was the message valuable?

_____

_____

_____

Notes:

_____

_____

_____

_____

Date:

Time:

Location:

Weather:

Moon Phase:

What kind of bird brought you a message/had a message for you today?

What were you doing when you noticed the messenger?

How were you feeling before the sighting?

Did the sighting evoke any immediate emotions? What are your first impressions about what the bird's message might be?

What thoughts came to mind about the sighting? Were you reminded of someone special or of an event in your past?

Were your feelings or mood transformed once you had the encounter?

_____

_____

_____

_____

Are there any situations in your life that might be connected to or
affected by the bird's message?

_____

_____

_____

_____

In what way does the bird's message resonate with you?

_____

_____

_____

_____

Follow Up: In hindsight, how did the sighting impact you, and how was
the message valuable?

_____

_____

_____

_____

Notes:

_____

_____

_____

_____

_____

Date:

Time:

Location:

Weather:

Moon Phase:

What kind of bird brought you a message/had a message for you today?

What were you doing when you noticed the messenger?

How were you feeling before the sighting?

Did the sighting evoke any immediate emotions? What are your first impressions about what the bird's message might be?

What thoughts came to mind about the sighting? Were you reminded of someone special or of an event in your past?

Were your feelings or mood transformed once you had the encounter?

_____

_____

_____

_____

Are there any situations in your life that might be connected to or affected by the bird's message?

_____

_____

_____

_____

In what way does the bird's message resonate with you?

_____

_____

_____

_____

Follow Up: In hindsight, how did the sighting impact you, and how was the message valuable?

_____

_____

_____

_____

Notes:

_____

_____

_____

_____

_____

Date:

Time:

Location:

Weather:

Moon Phase:

What kind of bird brought you a message/had a message for you today?

What were you doing when you noticed the messenger?

How were you feeling before the sighting?

Did the sighting evoke any immediate emotions? What are your first impressions about what the bird's message might be?

What thoughts came to mind about the sighting? Were you reminded of someone special or of an event in your past?

Were your feelings or mood transformed once you had the encounter?

_____

_____

_____

_____

Are there any situations in your life that might be connected to or affected by the bird's message?

_____

_____

_____

_____

In what way does the bird's message resonate with you?

_____

_____

_____

_____

Follow Up: In hindsight, how did the sighting impact you, and how was the message valuable?

_____

_____

_____

_____

Notes:

_____

_____

_____

_____

_____

Date:

Time:

Location:

Weather:

Moon Phase:

What kind of bird brought you a message/had a message for you today?

What were you doing when you noticed the messenger?

How were you feeling before the sighting?

Did the sighting evoke any immediate emotions? What are your first impressions about what the bird's message might be?

What thoughts came to mind about the sighting? Were you reminded of someone special or of an event in your past?

Were your feelings or mood transformed once you had the encounter?

_____

_____

_____

_____

Are there any situations in your life that might be connected to or affected by the bird's message?

_____

_____

_____

_____

In what way does the bird's message resonate with you?

_____

_____

_____

_____

Follow Up: In hindsight, how did the sighting impact you, and how was the message valuable?

_____

_____

_____

_____

Notes:

_____

_____

_____

_____

_____

Date: _____

Time: _____

Location: _____

Weather: _____

Moon Phase: _____

What kind of bird brought you a message/had a message for you today?

_____

_____

_____

What were you doing when you noticed the messenger?

_____

_____

_____

How were you feeling before the sighting?

_____

_____

_____

Did the sighting evoke any immediate emotions? What are your first impressions about what the bird's message might be?

_____

_____

_____

What thoughts came to mind about the sighting? Were you reminded of someone special or of an event in your past?

_____

_____

_____

Were your feelings or mood transformed once you had the encounter?

_____

_____

_____

_____

Are there any situations in your life that might be connected to or affected by the bird's message?

_____

_____

_____

_____

In what way does the bird's message resonate with you?

_____

_____

_____

_____

Follow Up: In hindsight, how did the sighting impact you, and how was the message valuable?

_____

_____

_____

_____

Notes:

_____

_____

_____

_____

Date:

Time:

Location:

Weather:

Moon Phase:

What kind of bird brought you a message/had a message for you today?

What were you doing when you noticed the messenger?

How were you feeling before the sighting?

Did the sighting evoke any immediate emotions? What are your first impressions about what the bird's message might be?

What thoughts came to mind about the sighting? Were you reminded of someone special or of an event in your past?

Were your feelings or mood transformed once you had the encounter?

_____

_____

_____

_____

Are there any situations in your life that might be connected to or affected by the bird's message?

_____

_____

_____

_____

In what way does the bird's message resonate with you?

_____

_____

_____

_____

Follow Up: In hindsight, how did the sighting impact you, and how was the message valuable?

_____

_____

_____

_____

Notes:

_____

_____

_____

_____

_____

Date:

Time:

Location:

Weather:

Moon Phase:

What kind of bird brought you a message/had a message for you today?

What were you doing when you noticed the messenger?

How were you feeling before the sighting?

Did the sighting evoke any immediate emotions? What are your first impressions about what the bird's message might be?

What thoughts came to mind about the sighting? Were you reminded of someone special or of an event in your past?

Were your feelings or mood transformed once you had the encounter?

_____

_____

_____

_____

Are there any situations in your life that might be connected to or affected by the bird's message?

_____

_____

_____

_____

In what way does the bird's message resonate with you?

_____

_____

_____

_____

Follow Up: In hindsight, how did the sighting impact you, and how was the message valuable?

_____

_____

_____

_____

Notes:

_____

_____

_____

_____

Date:

Time:

Location:

Weather:

Moon Phase:

What kind of bird brought you a message/had a message for you today?

What were you doing when you noticed the messenger?

How were you feeling before the sighting?

Did the sighting evoke any immediate emotions? What are your first impressions about what the bird's message might be?

What thoughts came to mind about the sighting? Were you reminded of someone special or of an event in your past?

Were your feelings or mood transformed once you had the encounter?

_____

_____

_____

_____

Are there any situations in your life that might be connected to or affected by the bird's message?

_____

_____

_____

_____

In what way does the bird's message resonate with you?

_____

_____

_____

_____

Follow Up: In hindsight, how did the sighting impact you, and how was the message valuable?

_____

_____

_____

_____

Notes:

_____

_____

_____

_____

_____

Date:

Time:

Location:

Weather:

Moon Phase:

What kind of bird brought you a message/had a message for you today?

What were you doing when you noticed the messenger?

How were you feeling before the sighting?

Did the sighting evoke any immediate emotions? What are your first impressions about what the bird's message might be?

What thoughts came to mind about the sighting? Were you reminded of someone special or of an event in your past?

Were your feelings or mood transformed once you had the encounter?

_____

_____

_____

_____

Are there any situations in your life that might be connected to or affected by the bird's message?

_____

_____

_____

_____

In what way does the bird's message resonate with you?

_____

_____

_____

_____

Follow Up: In hindsight, how did the sighting impact you, and how was the message valuable?

_____

_____

_____

_____

Notes:

_____

_____

_____

_____

_____

Date:

Time:

Location:

Weather:

Moon Phase:

What kind of bird brought you a message/had a message for you today?

What were you doing when you noticed the messenger?

How were you feeling before the sighting?

Did the sighting evoke any immediate emotions? What are your first impressions about what the bird's message might be?

What thoughts came to mind about the sighting? Were you reminded of someone special or of an event in your past?

Were your feelings or mood transformed once you had the encounter?

_____

_____

_____

_____

Are there any situations in your life that might be connected to or affected by the bird's message?

_____

_____

_____

_____

In what way does the bird's message resonate with you?

_____

_____

_____

_____

Follow Up: In hindsight, how did the sighting impact you, and how was the message valuable?

_____

_____

_____

_____

Notes:

_____

_____

_____

_____

Date:

Time:

Location:

Weather:

Moon Phase:

What kind of bird brought you a message/had a message for you today?

What were you doing when you noticed the messenger?

How were you feeling before the sighting?

Did the sighting evoke any immediate emotions? What are your first impressions about what the bird's message might be?

What thoughts came to mind about the sighting? Were you reminded of someone special or of an event in your past?

Were your feelings or mood transformed once you had the encounter?

_____

_____

_____

_____

Are there any situations in your life that might be connected to or
affected by the bird's message?

_____

_____

_____

_____

In what way does the bird's message resonate with you?

_____

_____

_____

_____

Follow Up: In hindsight, how did the sighting impact you, and how was
the message valuable?

_____

_____

_____

_____

Notes:

_____

_____

_____

_____

_____

Date:

Time:

Location:

Weather:

Moon Phase:

What kind of bird brought you a message/had a message for you today?

What were you doing when you noticed the messenger?

How were you feeling before the sighting?

Did the sighting evoke any immediate emotions? What are your first impressions about what the bird's message might be?

What thoughts came to mind about the sighting? Were you reminded of someone special or of an event in your past?

Were your feelings or mood transformed once you had the encounter?

_____

_____

_____

_____

Are there any situations in your life that might be connected to or affected by the bird's message?

_____

_____

_____

_____

In what way does the bird's message resonate with you?

_____

_____

_____

_____

Follow Up: In hindsight, how did the sighting impact you, and how was the message valuable?

_____

_____

_____

_____

Notes:

_____

_____

_____

_____

_____

Date:

Time:

Location:

Weather:

Moon Phase:

What kind of bird brought you a message/had a message for you today?

What were you doing when you noticed the messenger?

How were you feeling before the sighting?

Did the sighting evoke any immediate emotions? What are your first impressions about what the bird's message might be?

What thoughts came to mind about the sighting? Were you reminded of someone special or of an event in your past?

Were your feelings or mood transformed once you had the encounter?

_____

_____

_____

_____

Are there any situations in your life that might be connected to or affected by the bird's message?

_____

_____

_____

_____

In what way does the bird's message resonate with you?

_____

_____

_____

_____

Follow Up: In hindsight, how did the sighting impact you, and how was the message valuable?

_____

_____

_____

_____

Notes:

_____

_____

_____

_____

Date: _____

Time: _____

Location: _____

Weather: _____

Moon Phase: _____

What kind of bird brought you a message/had a message for you today?

_____

_____

What were you doing when you noticed the messenger?

_____

_____

_____

How were you feeling before the sighting?

_____

_____

Did the sighting evoke any immediate emotions? What are your first impressions about what the bird's message might be?

_____

_____

_____

What thoughts came to mind about the sighting? Were you reminded of someone special or of an event in your past?

_____

_____

_____

Were your feelings or mood transformed once you had the encounter?

_____

_____

_____

_____

Are there any situations in your life that might be connected to or affected by the bird's message?

_____

_____

_____

_____

In what way does the bird's message resonate with you?

_____

_____

_____

_____

Follow Up: In hindsight, how did the sighting impact you, and how was the message valuable?

_____

_____

_____

_____

Notes:

_____

_____

_____

_____

_____

Date:

Time:

Location:

Weather:

Moon Phase:

What kind of bird brought you a message/had a message for you today?

What were you doing when you noticed the messenger?

How were you feeling before the sighting?

Did the sighting evoke any immediate emotions? What are your first impressions about what the bird's message might be?

What thoughts came to mind about the sighting? Were you reminded of someone special or of an event in your past?

Were your feelings or mood transformed once you had the encounter?

_____

_____

_____

_____

Are there any situations in your life that might be connected to or
affected by the bird's message?

_____

_____

_____

_____

In what way does the bird's message resonate with you?

_____

_____

_____

_____

Follow Up: In hindsight, how did the sighting impact you, and how was
the message valuable?

_____

_____

_____

_____

Notes:

_____

_____

_____

_____

_____

Date:

Time:

Location:

Weather:

Moon Phase:

What kind of bird brought you a message/had a message for you today?

What were you doing when you noticed the messenger?

How were you feeling before the sighting?

Did the sighting evoke any immediate emotions? What are your first impressions about what the bird's message might be?

What thoughts came to mind about the sighting? Were you reminded of someone special or of an event in your past?

Were your feelings or mood transformed once you had the encounter?

_____

_____

_____

_____

Are there any situations in your life that might be connected to or affected by the bird's message?

_____

_____

_____

_____

In what way does the bird's message resonate with you?

_____

_____

_____

_____

Follow Up: In hindsight, how did the sighting impact you, and how was the message valuable?

_____

_____

_____

_____

Notes:

_____

_____

_____

_____

_____

Date:

Time:

Location:

Weather:

Moon Phase:

What kind of bird brought you a message/had a message for you today?

What were you doing when you noticed the messenger?

How were you feeling before the sighting?

Did the sighting evoke any immediate emotions? What are your first impressions about what the bird's message might be?

What thoughts came to mind about the sighting? Were you reminded of someone special or of an event in your past?

Were your feelings or mood transformed once you had the encounter?

_____

_____

_____

_____

Are there any situations in your life that might be connected to or affected by the bird's message?

_____

_____

_____

_____

In what way does the bird's message resonate with you?

_____

_____

_____

_____

Follow Up: In hindsight, how did the sighting impact you, and how was the message valuable?

_____

_____

_____

Notes:

_____

_____

_____

_____

_____

Date:

Time:

Location:

Weather:

Moon Phase:

What kind of bird brought you a message/had a message for you today?

_____

_____

_____

What were you doing when you noticed the messenger?

_____

_____

_____

How were you feeling before the sighting?

_____

_____

Did the sighting evoke any immediate emotions? What are your first impressions about what the bird's message might be?

_____

_____

_____

What thoughts came to mind about the sighting? Were you reminded of someone special or of an event in your past?

_____

_____

_____

_____

Were your feelings or mood transformed once you had the encounter?

_____

_____

_____

_____

Are there any situations in your life that might be connected to or
affected by the bird's message?

_____

_____

_____

_____

In what way does the bird's message resonate with you?

_____

_____

_____

_____

Follow Up: In hindsight, how did the sighting impact you, and how was
the message valuable?

_____

_____

_____

_____

Notes:

_____

_____

_____

_____

_____

Date:

Time:

Location:

Weather:

Moon Phase:

What kind of bird brought you a message/had a message for you today?

What were you doing when you noticed the messenger?

How were you feeling before the sighting?

Did the sighting evoke any immediate emotions? What are your first impressions about what the bird's message might be?

What thoughts came to mind about the sighting? Were you reminded of someone special or of an event in your past?

Were your feelings or mood transformed once you had the encounter?

_____

_____

_____

_____

Are there any situations in your life that might be connected to or affected by the bird's message?

_____

_____

_____

_____

In what way does the bird's message resonate with you?

_____

_____

_____

_____

Follow Up: In hindsight, how did the sighting impact you, and how was the message valuable?

_____

_____

_____

_____

Notes:

_____

_____

_____

_____

Date:

Time:

Location:

Weather:

Moon Phase:

What kind of bird brought you a message/had a message for you today?

What were you doing when you noticed the messenger?

How were you feeling before the sighting?

Did the sighting evoke any immediate emotions? What are your first impressions about what the bird's message might be?

What thoughts came to mind about the sighting? Were you reminded of someone special or of an event in your past?

Were your feelings or mood transformed once you had the encounter?

_____

_____

_____

_____

Are there any situations in your life that might be connected to or affected by the bird's message?

_____

_____

_____

_____

In what way does the bird's message resonate with you?

_____

_____

_____

_____

Follow Up: In hindsight, how did the sighting impact you, and how was the message valuable?

_____

_____

_____

_____

Notes:

_____

_____

_____

_____

_____

Date:

Time:

Location:

Weather:

Moon Phase:

What kind of bird brought you a message/had a message for you today?

What were you doing when you noticed the messenger?

How were you feeling before the sighting?

Did the sighting evoke any immediate emotions? What are your first impressions about what the bird's message might be?

What thoughts came to mind about the sighting? Were you reminded of someone special or of an event in your past?

Were your feelings or mood transformed once you had the encounter?

_____

_____

_____

_____

Are there any situations in your life that might be connected to or affected by the bird's message?

_____

_____

_____

_____

In what way does the bird's message resonate with you?

_____

_____

_____

_____

Follow Up: In hindsight, how did the sighting impact you, and how was the message valuable?

_____

_____

_____

_____

Notes:

_____

_____

_____

_____

Date:

Time:

Location:

Weather:

Moon Phase:

What kind of bird brought you a message/had a message for you today?

_____

_____

_____

What were you doing when you noticed the messenger?

_____

_____

_____

How were you feeling before the sighting?

_____

_____

_____

Did the sighting evoke any immediate emotions? What are your first impressions about what the bird's message might be?

_____

_____

_____

What thoughts came to mind about the sighting? Were you reminded of someone special or of an event in your past?

_____

_____

_____

_____

Were your feelings or mood transformed once you had the encounter?

_____

_____

_____

_____

Are there any situations in your life that might be connected to or affected by the bird's message?

_____

_____

_____

_____

In what way does the bird's message resonate with you?

_____

_____

_____

_____

Follow Up: In hindsight, how did the sighting impact you, and how was the message valuable?

_____

_____

_____

_____

Notes:

_____

_____

_____

_____

_____

Date:

Time:

Location:

Weather:

Moon Phase:

What kind of bird brought you a message/had a message for you today?

What were you doing when you noticed the messenger?

How were you feeling before the sighting?

Did the sighting evoke any immediate emotions? What are your first impressions about what the bird's message might be?

What thoughts came to mind about the sighting? Were you reminded of someone special or of an event in your past?

Were your feelings or mood transformed once you had the encounter?

_____

_____

_____

_____

Are there any situations in your life that might be connected to or affected by the bird's message?

_____

_____

_____

_____

In what way does the bird's message resonate with you?

_____

_____

_____

_____

Follow Up: In hindsight, how did the sighting impact you, and how was the message valuable?

_____

_____

_____

_____

Notes:

_____

_____

_____

_____

Date:

Time:

Location:

Weather:

Moon Phase:

What kind of bird brought you a message/had a message for you today?

What were you doing when you noticed the messenger?

How were you feeling before the sighting?

Did the sighting evoke any immediate emotions? What are your first impressions about what the bird's message might be?

What thoughts came to mind about the sighting? Were you reminded of someone special or of an event in your past?

Were your feelings or mood transformed once you had the encounter?

_____

_____

_____

_____

Are there any situations in your life that might be connected to or
affected by the bird's message?

_____

_____

_____

_____

In what way does the bird's message resonate with you?

_____

_____

_____

_____

Follow Up: In hindsight, how did the sighting impact you, and how was
the message valuable?

_____

_____

_____

_____

Notes:

_____

_____

_____

_____

Date:

Time:

Location:

Weather:

Moon Phase:

What kind of bird brought you a message/had a message for you today?

What were you doing when you noticed the messenger?

How were you feeling before the sighting?

Did the sighting evoke any immediate emotions? What are your first impressions about what the bird's message might be?

What thoughts came to mind about the sighting? Were you reminded of someone special or of an event in your past?

Were your feelings or mood transformed once you had the encounter?

_____

_____

_____

_____

Are there any situations in your life that might be connected to or
affected by the bird's message?

_____

_____

_____

_____

In what way does the bird's message resonate with you?

_____

_____

_____

_____

Follow Up: In hindsight, how did the sighting impact you, and how was
the message valuable?

_____

_____

_____

_____

Notes:
_____

_____

_____

_____

_____

Date:

Time:

Location:

Weather:

Moon Phase:

What kind of bird brought you a message/had a message for you today?

_____

_____

What were you doing when you noticed the messenger?

_____

_____

How were you feeling before the sighting?

_____

_____

Did the sighting evoke any immediate emotions? What are your first impressions about what the bird's message might be?

_____

_____

What thoughts came to mind about the sighting? Were you reminded of someone special or of an event in your past?

_____

_____

_____

Were your feelings or mood transformed once you had the encounter?

_____

_____

_____

_____

Are there any situations in your life that might be connected to or affected by the bird's message?

_____

_____

_____

_____

In what way does the bird's message resonate with you?

_____

_____

_____

_____

Follow Up: In hindsight, how did the sighting impact you, and how was the message valuable?

_____

_____

_____

_____

Notes:

_____

_____

_____

_____

_____

_____

Date:

Time:

Location:

Weather:

Moon Phase:

What kind of bird brought you a message/had a message for you today?

What were you doing when you noticed the messenger?

How were you feeling before the sighting?

Did the sighting evoke any immediate emotions? What are your first impressions about what the bird's message might be?

What thoughts came to mind about the sighting? Were you reminded of someone special or of an event in your past?

Were your feelings or mood transformed once you had the encounter?

_____

_____

_____

_____

Are there any situations in your life that might be connected to or affected by the bird's message?

_____

_____

_____

_____

In what way does the bird's message resonate with you?

_____

_____

_____

_____

Follow Up: In hindsight, how did the sighting impact you, and how was the message valuable?

_____

_____

_____

_____

Notes:

_____

_____

_____

_____

_____

Date: _____

Time: _____

Location: _____

Weather: _____

Moon Phase: _____

What kind of bird brought you a message/had a message for you today?

_____

_____

_____

What were you doing when you noticed the messenger?

_____

_____

_____

How were you feeling before the sighting?

_____

_____

_____

Did the sighting evoke any immediate emotions? What are your first impressions about what the bird's message might be?

_____

_____

_____

What thoughts came to mind about the sighting? Were you reminded of someone special or of an event in your past?

_____

_____

_____

_____

Were your feelings or mood transformed once you had the encounter?

_____

_____

_____

_____

Are there any situations in your life that might be connected to or affected by the bird's message?

_____

_____

_____

_____

In what way does the bird's message resonate with you?

_____

_____

_____

_____

Follow Up: In hindsight, how did the sighting impact you, and how was the message valuable?

_____

_____

_____

_____

Notes:

_____

_____

_____

_____

_____

Date:

Time:

Location:

Weather:

Moon Phase:

What kind of bird brought you a message/had a message for you today?

What were you doing when you noticed the messenger?

How were you feeling before the sighting?

Did the sighting evoke any immediate emotions? What are your first impressions about what the bird's message might be?

What thoughts came to mind about the sighting? Were you reminded of someone special or of an event in your past?

Were your feelings or mood transformed once you had the encounter?

_____

_____

_____

_____

Are there any situations in your life that might be connected to or affected by the bird's message?

_____

_____

_____

_____

In what way does the bird's message resonate with you?

_____

_____

_____

_____

Follow Up: In hindsight, how did the sighting impact you, and how was the message valuable?

_____

_____

_____

_____

Notes:

_____

_____

_____

_____

_____

Date:

Time:

Location:

Weather:

Moon Phase:

What kind of bird brought you a message/had a message for you today?

What were you doing when you noticed the messenger?

How were you feeling before the sighting?

Did the sighting evoke any immediate emotions? What are your first impressions about what the bird's message might be?

What thoughts came to mind about the sighting? Were you reminded of someone special or of an event in your past?

Were your feelings or mood transformed once you had the encounter?

_____

_____

_____

_____

Are there any situations in your life that might be connected to or affected by the bird's message?

_____

_____

_____

_____

In what way does the bird's message resonate with you?

_____

_____

_____

_____

Follow Up: In hindsight, how did the sighting impact you, and how was the message valuable?

_____

_____

_____

_____

Notes:

_____

_____

_____

_____

_____

Date:

Time:

Location:

Weather:

Moon Phase:

What kind of bird brought you a message/had a message for you today?

What were you doing when you noticed the messenger?

How were you feeling before the sighting?

Did the sighting evoke any immediate emotions? What are your first impressions about what the bird's message might be?

What thoughts came to mind about the sighting? Were you reminded of someone special or of an event in your past?

Were your feelings or mood transformed once you had the encounter?

_____

_____

_____

_____

Are there any situations in your life that might be connected to or affected by the bird's message?

_____

_____

_____

_____

In what way does the bird's message resonate with you?

_____

_____

_____

_____

Follow Up: In hindsight, how did the sighting impact you, and how was the message valuable?

_____

_____

_____

Notes:

_____

_____

_____

_____

Date:

Time:

Location:

Weather:

Moon Phase:

What kind of bird brought you a message/had a message for you today?

What were you doing when you noticed the messenger?

How were you feeling before the sighting?

Did the sighting evoke any immediate emotions? What are your first impressions about what the bird's message might be?

What thoughts came to mind about the sighting? Were you reminded of someone special or of an event in your past?

Were your feelings or mood transformed once you had the encounter?

_____

_____

_____

Are there any situations in your life that might be connected to or affected by the bird's message?

_____

_____

_____

In what way does the bird's message resonate with you?

_____

_____

_____

Follow Up: In hindsight, how did the sighting impact you, and how was the message valuable?

_____

_____

_____

Notes:

_____

_____

_____

_____

Date: _____

Time: _____

Location: _____

Weather: _____

Moon Phase: _____

What kind of bird brought you a message/had a message for you today?

_____

_____

_____

What were you doing when you noticed the messenger?

_____

_____

_____

How were you feeling before the sighting?

_____

_____

_____

Did the sighting evoke any immediate emotions? What are your first impressions about what the bird's message might be?

_____

_____

_____

What thoughts came to mind about the sighting? Were you reminded of someone special or of an event in your past?

_____

_____

_____

Were your feelings or mood transformed once you had the encounter?

_____

_____

_____

_____

Are there any situations in your life that might be connected to or affected by the bird's message?

_____

_____

_____

_____

In what way does the bird's message resonate with you?

_____

_____

_____

Follow Up: In hindsight, how did the sighting impact you, and how was the message valuable?

_____

_____

_____

_____

Notes:

_____

_____

_____

_____

Date:

Time:

Location:

Weather:

Moon Phase:

What kind of bird brought you a message/had a message for you today?

What were you doing when you noticed the messenger?

How were you feeling before the sighting?

Did the sighting evoke any immediate emotions? What are your first impressions about what the bird's message might be?

What thoughts came to mind about the sighting? Were you reminded of someone special or of an event in your past?

Were your feelings or mood transformed once you had the encounter?

_____

_____

_____

_____

Are there any situations in your life that might be connected to or affected by the bird's message?

_____

_____

_____

_____

In what way does the bird's message resonate with you?

_____

_____

_____

_____

Follow Up: In hindsight, how did the sighting impact you, and how was the message valuable?

_____

_____

_____

_____

Notes:

_____

_____

_____

_____

_____

Date: _____

Time: _____

Location: _____

Weather: _____

Moon Phase: _____

What kind of bird brought you a message/had a message for you today?

_____

_____

_____

What were you doing when you noticed the messenger?

_____

_____

_____

How were you feeling before the sighting?

_____

_____

_____

Did the sighting evoke any immediate emotions? What are your first impressions about what the bird's message might be?

_____

_____

_____

What thoughts came to mind about the sighting? Were you reminded of someone special or of an event in your past?

_____

_____

_____

Were your feelings or mood transformed once you had the encounter?

_____

_____

_____

_____

Are there any situations in your life that might be connected to or affected by the bird's message?

_____

_____

_____

_____

In what way does the bird's message resonate with you?

_____

_____

_____

_____

Follow Up: In hindsight, how did the sighting impact you, and how was the message valuable?

_____

_____

_____

_____

Notes:

_____

_____

_____

_____

_____

Date:

Time:

Location:

Weather:

Moon Phase:

What kind of bird brought you a message/had a message for you today?

What were you doing when you noticed the messenger?

How were you feeling before the sighting?

Did the sighting evoke any immediate emotions? What are your first impressions about what the bird's message might be?

What thoughts came to mind about the sighting? Were you reminded of someone special or of an event in your past?

Were your feelings or mood transformed once you had the encounter?

_____

_____

_____

_____

Are there any situations in your life that might be connected to or
affected by the bird's message?

_____

_____

_____

In what way does the bird's message resonate with you?

_____

_____

_____

Follow Up: In hindsight, how did the sighting impact you, and how was
the message valuable?

_____

_____

_____

_____

Notes:

_____

_____

_____

_____

Date:

Time:

Location:

Weather:

Moon Phase:

What kind of bird brought you a message/had a message for you today?

What were you doing when you noticed the messenger?

How were you feeling before the sighting?

Did the sighting evoke any immediate emotions? What are your first impressions about what the bird's message might be?

What thoughts came to mind about the sighting? Were you reminded of someone special or of an event in your past?

Were your feelings or mood transformed once you had the encounter?

_____

_____

_____

_____

Are there any situations in your life that might be connected to or affected by the bird's message?

_____

_____

_____

_____

In what way does the bird's message resonate with you?

_____

_____

_____

_____

Follow Up: In hindsight, how did the sighting impact you, and how was the message valuable?

_____

_____

_____

_____

Notes: _____

_____

_____

_____

_____

Date:

Time:

Location:

Weather:

Moon Phase:

What kind of bird brought you a message/had a message for you today?

What were you doing when you noticed the messenger?

How were you feeling before the sighting?

Did the sighting evoke any immediate emotions? What are your first impressions about what the bird's message might be?

What thoughts came to mind about the sighting? Were you reminded of someone special or of an event in your past?

Were your feelings or mood transformed once you had the encounter?

_____

_____

_____

_____

Are there any situations in your life that might be connected to or affected by the bird's message?

_____

_____

_____

_____

In what way does the bird's message resonate with you?

_____

_____

_____

_____

Follow Up: In hindsight, how did the sighting impact you, and how was the message valuable?

_____

_____

_____

_____

Notes:

_____

_____

_____

_____

_____

Date:

Time:

Location:

Weather:

Moon Phase:

What kind of bird brought you a message/had a message for you today?

_____

_____

_____

What were you doing when you noticed the messenger?

_____

_____

_____

How were you feeling before the sighting?

_____

_____

_____

Did the sighting evoke any immediate emotions? What are your first impressions about what the bird's message might be?

_____

_____

_____

What thoughts came to mind about the sighting? Were you reminded of someone special or of an event in your past?

_____

_____

_____

_____

Were your feelings or mood transformed once you had the encounter?

_____

_____

_____

_____

Are there any situations in your life that might be connected to or affected by the bird's message?

_____

_____

_____

_____

In what way does the bird's message resonate with you?

_____

_____

_____

_____

Follow Up: In hindsight, how did the sighting impact you, and how was the message valuable?

_____

_____

_____

_____

Notes:

_____

_____

_____

_____

_____

Date:

Time:

Location:

Weather:

Moon Phase:

What kind of bird brought you a message/had a message for you today?

What were you doing when you noticed the messenger?

How were you feeling before the sighting?

Did the sighting evoke any immediate emotions? What are your first impressions about what the bird's message might be?

What thoughts came to mind about the sighting? Were you reminded of someone special or of an event in your past?

Were your feelings or mood transformed once you had the encounter?

_____

_____

_____

_____

Are there any situations in your life that might be connected to or affected by the bird's message?

_____

_____

_____

_____

In what way does the bird's message resonate with you?

_____

_____

_____

_____

Follow Up: In hindsight, how did the sighting impact you, and how was the message valuable?

_____

_____

_____

_____

Notes:

_____

_____

_____

_____

_____

Date:

Time:

Location:

Weather:

Moon Phase:

What kind of bird brought you a message/had a message for you today?

What were you doing when you noticed the messenger?

How were you feeling before the sighting?

Did the sighting evoke any immediate emotions? What are your first impressions about what the bird's message might be?

What thoughts came to mind about the sighting? Were you reminded of someone special or of an event in your past?

Were your feelings or mood transformed once you had the encounter?

_____

_____

_____

_____

Are there any situations in your life that might be connected to or
affected by the bird's message?

_____

_____

_____

_____

In what way does the bird's message resonate with you?

_____

_____

_____

_____

Follow Up: In hindsight, how did the sighting impact you, and how was
the message valuable?

_____

_____

_____

_____

Notes:

_____

_____

_____

_____

_____

Date:

Time:

Location:

Weather:

Moon Phase:

What kind of bird brought you a message/had a message for you today?

What were you doing when you noticed the messenger?

How were you feeling before the sighting?

Did the sighting evoke any immediate emotions? What are your first impressions about what the bird's message might be?

What thoughts came to mind about the sighting? Were you reminded of someone special or of an event in your past?

Were your feelings or mood transformed once you had the encounter?

_____

_____

_____

_____

Are there any situations in your life that might be connected to or affected by the bird's message?

_____

_____

_____

_____

In what way does the bird's message resonate with you?

_____

_____

_____

_____

Follow Up: In hindsight, how did the sighting impact you, and how was the message valuable?

_____

_____

_____

_____

Notes:

_____

_____

_____

_____

_____

Date:

Time:

Location:

Weather:

Moon Phase:

What kind of bird brought you a message/had a message for you today?

What were you doing when you noticed the messenger?

How were you feeling before the sighting?

Did the sighting evoke any immediate emotions? What are your first impressions about what the bird's message might be?

What thoughts came to mind about the sighting? Were you reminded of someone special or of an event in your past?

Were your feelings or mood transformed once you had the encounter?

_____

_____

_____

_____

Are there any situations in your life that might be connected to or affected by the bird's message?

_____

_____

_____

_____

In what way does the bird's message resonate with you?

_____

_____

_____

_____

Follow Up: In hindsight, how did the sighting impact you, and how was the message valuable?

_____

_____

_____

_____

Notes:

_____

_____

_____

_____

_____

Date:

Time:

Location:

Weather:

Moon Phase:

What kind of bird brought you a message/had a message for you today?

What were you doing when you noticed the messenger?

How were you feeling before the sighting?

Did the sighting evoke any immediate emotions? What are your first impressions about what the bird's message might be?

What thoughts came to mind about the sighting? Were you reminded of someone special or of an event in your past?

Were your feelings or mood transformed once you had the encounter?

_____

_____

_____

_____

Are there any situations in your life that might be connected to or affected by the bird's message?

_____

_____

_____

_____

In what way does the bird's message resonate with you?

_____

_____

_____

_____

Follow Up: In hindsight, how did the sighting impact you, and how was the message valuable?

_____

_____

_____

_____

Notes:

_____

_____

_____

_____

_____

Date:

Time:

Location:

Weather:

Moon Phase:

What kind of bird brought you a message/had a message for you today?

What were you doing when you noticed the messenger?

How were you feeling before the sighting?

Did the sighting evoke any immediate emotions? What are your first impressions about what the bird's message might be?

What thoughts came to mind about the sighting? Were you reminded of someone special or of an event in your past?

Were your feelings or mood transformed once you had the encounter?

_____

_____

_____

_____

Are there any situations in your life that might be connected to or affected by the bird's message?

_____

_____

_____

_____

In what way does the bird's message resonate with you?

_____

_____

_____

_____

Follow Up: In hindsight, how did the sighting impact you, and how was the message valuable?

_____

_____

_____

_____

Notes:

_____

_____

_____

_____

_____

Date:

Time:

Location:

Weather:

Moon Phase:

What kind of bird brought you a message/had a message for you today?

What were you doing when you noticed the messenger?

How were you feeling before the sighting?

Did the sighting evoke any immediate emotions? What are your first impressions about what the bird's message might be?

What thoughts came to mind about the sighting? Were you reminded of someone special or of an event in your past?

Were your feelings or mood transformed once you had the encounter?

_____

_____

_____

_____

Are there any situations in your life that might be connected to or affected by the bird's message?

_____

_____

_____

_____

In what way does the bird's message resonate with you?

_____

_____

_____

_____

Follow Up: In hindsight, how did the sighting impact you, and how was the message valuable?

_____

_____

_____

_____

Notes:

_____

_____

_____

_____

_____

Date:

Time:

Location:

Weather:

Moon Phase:

What kind of bird brought you a message/had a message for you today?

What were you doing when you noticed the messenger?

How were you feeling before the sighting?

Did the sighting evoke any immediate emotions? What are your first impressions about what the bird's message might be?

What thoughts came to mind about the sighting? Were you reminded of someone special or of an event in your past?

Were your feelings or mood transformed once you had the encounter?

_____

_____

_____

_____

Are there any situations in your life that might be connected to or affected by the bird's message?

_____

_____

_____

_____

In what way does the bird's message resonate with you?

_____

_____

_____

_____

Follow Up: In hindsight, how did the sighting impact you, and how was the message valuable?

_____

_____

_____

_____

Notes:

_____

_____

_____

_____

_____

Date:

Time:

Location:

Weather:

Moon Phase:

What kind of bird brought you a message/had a message for you today?

What were you doing when you noticed the messenger?

How were you feeling before the sighting?

Did the sighting evoke any immediate emotions? What are your first impressions about what the bird's message might be?

What thoughts came to mind about the sighting? Were you reminded of someone special or of an event in your past?

Were your feelings or mood transformed once you had the encounter?

_____

_____

_____

_____

Are there any situations in your life that might be connected to or affected by the bird's message?

_____

_____

_____

_____

In what way does the bird's message resonate with you?

_____

_____

_____

_____

Follow Up: In hindsight, how did the sighting impact you, and how was the message valuable?

_____

_____

_____

_____

Notes:

_____

_____

_____

_____

_____

Date:

Time:

Location:

Weather:

Moon Phase:

What kind of bird brought you a message/had a message for you today?

What were you doing when you noticed the messenger?

How were you feeling before the sighting?

Did the sighting evoke any immediate emotions? What are your first impressions about what the bird's message might be?

What thoughts came to mind about the sighting? Were you reminded of someone special or of an event in your past?

Were your feelings or mood transformed once you had the encounter?

_____

_____

_____

_____

Are there any situations in your life that might be connected to or
affected by the bird's message?

_____

_____

_____

_____

In what way does the bird's message resonate with you?

_____

_____

_____

_____

Follow Up: In hindsight, how did the sighting impact you, and how was
the message valuable?

_____

_____

_____

_____

Notes:

_____

_____

_____

_____

_____

Date:

Time:

Location:

Weather:

Moon Phase:

What kind of bird brought you a message/had a message for you today?

What were you doing when you noticed the messenger?

How were you feeling before the sighting?

Did the sighting evoke any immediate emotions? What are your first impressions about what the bird's message might be?

What thoughts came to mind about the sighting? Were you reminded of someone special or of an event in your past?

Were your feelings or mood transformed once you had the encounter?

_____

_____

_____

_____

Are there any situations in your life that might be connected to or affected by the bird's message?

_____

_____

_____

_____

In what way does the bird's message resonate with you?

_____

_____

_____

_____

Follow Up: In hindsight, how did the sighting impact you, and how was the message valuable?

_____

_____

_____

_____

Notes:

_____

_____

_____

_____

_____

Date:

Time:

Location:

Weather:

Moon Phase:

What kind of bird brought you a message/had a message for you today?

What were you doing when you noticed the messenger?

How were you feeling before the sighting?

Did the sighting evoke any immediate emotions? What are your first impressions about what the bird's message might be?

What thoughts came to mind about the sighting? Were you reminded of someone special or of an event in your past?

Were your feelings or mood transformed once you had the encounter?

_____

_____

_____

_____

Are there any situations in your life that might be connected to or affected by the bird's message?

_____

_____

_____

_____

In what way does the bird's message resonate with you?

_____

_____

_____

_____

Follow Up: In hindsight, how did the sighting impact you, and how was the message valuable?

_____

_____

_____

_____

Notes:

_____

_____

_____

_____

Bird Reference

For your reference, here are images of the sixty-two birds most often seen in North America, along with a short description of each bird's spiritual symbology. This section should help you identify the messengers that appear to you and will help you on the path toward understanding their significance in your life. For more detailed information on and images of each bird, please refer to *Birds: A Spiritual Field Guide*, this journal's companion text.

ALBATROSS. Represents conservation of energy, trust in yourself, family, and heritage.

BLACKBIRD. Represents defense, standing up for your rights or beliefs, hidden potential, and hidden motives.

BLUE JAY. Represents family bonds, social networks, communication, loyalty, and fearlessness.

BLUEBIRD. Represents happiness, joy, serendipity, hearth and home, gentleness, peace, tranquility, hope.

CARDINAL. Represents leadership, self-worth, confidence, creativity, energy, and activity.

CHICKADEE. Represents industry, leadership, unity, activity, playfulness, adaptability, and optimism.

CORMORANT. Represents abundance and commitment.

CRANE. Represents longevity, success, watchfulness, justice, and fidelity.

CROW. Represents death, prophecy, change, play, and innovation.

CUCKOO. Represents prophecy, the Otherworld, change, transformation, fertility, and long life.

DOVE. Represents peace, love, patience, grace, hope, and purity.

DUCK. Represents emotional balance, transition, wisdom, and partnership.

EAGLE. Represents renewal, perception, power, leadership, and longevity.

EGRET. Represents stability and beauty.

FALCON. Represents perception, efficiency, power, and balance.

FINCH. Represents activity and energy.

FLAMINGO. Represents grace, thoroughness, cooperation, and balance.

GOLDFINCH. Represents joy, happiness, health, abundance, and prosperity.

GOOSE. Represents fecundity, protection, domesticity, teamwork, and travel.

GRACKLE. Represents determination, aggression, and illusion.

GROUSE. Represents movement, stillness, and the life cycle.

GULL. Represents balance, adaptability, and freedom.

HAWK. Represents health, protection, strength, perception, and observation.

HERON. Represents patience, self-reliance, observation, focus, and concentration.

HUMMINGBIRD. Represents joy, energy management, sweetness, and vitality.

IBIS. Represents wisdom, knowledge, and a connection to the sacred.

KESTREL. Represents watchfulness and power in small packages.

KINGFISHER. Represents precision, timing, good fortune, peace, and calm.

LARK. Represents joy, celebration, and playfulness.

LOON. Represents dreams, peace, and tranquility.

MAGPIE. Represents hoarding, distraction, communication, and balance between extremes.

MOCKINGBIRD. Represents reflection, communication, humor, and improvisation.

NIGHTHAWK. Represents adaptability, agility, and transition.

NUTHATCH. Represents adaptability, new viewpoints, and preparation for the future.

ORIOLE. Represents new projects, creativity, happiness and cheer, domesticity, and positive energy.

OSPREY. Represents perception, abundance, and success.

OWL. Represents keen sight, excellent hearing, wisdom, and prophecy.

PARAKEET. Represents play, reflection, and captivity.

PARTRIDGE. Represents fertility, camouflage, and abundance.

PELICAN. Represents devotion, self-sacrifice, charity, and strong parenting.

PETREL. Represents energy conservation and faith.

PIGEON. Represents community, cooperation, and communication.

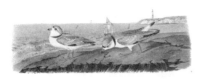

PLOVER. Represents preparation, advance planning, and travel.

PUFFIN. Represents parenting, being true to yourself, and playing to your strengths.

QUAIL. Represents caution, fertility, fecundity, courage, tenacity, and nourishment.

RAVEN. Represents insight, play, appreciation of luxury, prophecy, and death.

ROBIN. Represents new beginnings, celebration, compassion, and good fortune.

SANDPIPER. Represents scavenging, quickness, balance, and a willingness to seek what is below the surface.

SPARROW. Represents companionship, adaptability, sharing, and self-worth.

STARLING. Represents community and communication.

STORK. Represents fidelity, acceptance, and familial relationships and responsibilities.

SWALLOW. Represents hope, renewal, hearth and home, and courage.

SWAN. Represents transformation, grace, beauty, compassion, fidelity, and love.

SWIFT. Represents speed, agility, travel, movement, and hearth and home.

THRUSH. Represents voice, message, beauty, and commitment.

TURKEY. Represents abundance, gratitude, nourishment, and wisdom.

VULTURE. Represents death, disposal, and improvement of health.

WAXWING. Represents sharing, affection, and gluttony.

WHIP-POOR-WILL. Represents voice over appearance, and lunar energy.

WOODPECKER. Represents determination, focus, and safe passage.

WREN. Represents family, home, balance, strength, and courage.

YELLOW WARBLER. Represents joy, celebration, and creativity.